# On My Own

## A Guide To Finding Yourself Through Female Solo Travel

By
Sandra Denise Parker

First published by Ultimate World Publishing 2023
Copyright © 2023 Sandra Parker

ISBN

Paperback: 978-1-922982-56-8
Ebook: 978-1-922982-57-5

Sandra Parker has asserted her rights under the Copyright, Designs and Patents Act 1988 to be identified as the author of this work. The information in this book is based on the author's experiences and opinions. The publisher specifically disclaims responsibility for any adverse consequences which may result from use of the information contained herein. Permission to use information has been sought by the author. Any breaches will be rectified in further editions of the book.

All rights reserved. No part of this publication may be reproduced, stored in or introduced into a retrieval system, or transmitted in any form, or by any means (electronic, mechanical, photocopying, recording or otherwise) without the prior written permission of the author. Any person who does any unauthorized act in relation to this publication may be liable to criminal prosecution and civil claims for damages. Enquiries should be made through the publisher.

**Cover design:** Sandra Denise Parker
**Layout and typesetting:** Ultimate World Publishing
**Editor:** Rebecca Low

Ultimate World Publishing
Diamond Creek,
Victoria Australia 3089
www.writeabook.com.au

I dedicate this book to my children, Chanyra and Winston.

My beautiful granddaughters Brooke and Bailie.

You are all my heart strings. Everything I do is for you.

To my mother and my father who are
now my guardian angels

# Watching over me.
# I love and miss you so much.

# Contents

| | |
|---|---|
| Preface | 1 |
| CHAPTER 1: How It All Began | 5 |
| CHAPTER 2: What's In It For Me? | 10 |
| CHAPTER 3: Learning From My Journey | 20 |
| CHAPTER 4: Loneliness And Solo-friendly Destinations | 31 |
| CHAPTER 5: Where Do I Start? | 38 |
| CHAPTER 6: Planning Is Definitely A Process | 44 |
| CHAPTER 7: Solo Cruising | 61 |
| CHAPTER 8: Safety Is Always First | 68 |
| CHAPTER 9: It's All About The Money | 76 |
| CHAPTER 10: The Packing Saga And Luggage Wars | 82 |
| CHAPTER 11: Let's Go Take Pictures And Explore | 93 |
| CHAPTER 12: You're On Vacation | 102 |
| About The Author | 105 |
| Acknowledgments | 107 |

# Preface

*The woman who follows the crowd will usually go no further than the crowd. The woman who walks alone is likely to find herself in places no one has ever been before."*
**Albert Einstein**

People often ask why I travel solo. I love to travel. That's it. History, architecture and exploring different cultures all around the globe is my passion. I love meeting people and sharing experiences with them, often making new and lasting friendships. Most of all, I like how solo travel helped me to find and love myself. Traveling is my joy. It's therapy for me. I'm a nurse administrator and a life coach. I problem-solve all day in both my professions. I love what I do, but travel helps me release all the tension and toxins I accumulate every day at work.

Vacations are a necessity for me, I come back refreshed, a better me and ready to serve again. Other than my yearly vacation with my family, I have no time to wait for people to decide if they're going to accompany me. What amazed me was the fascination other people had about my travel adventures. They loved the photographs, the stories that went with them, and the fact that I had no fear traveling solo. Some of them have never left the state or country, so they traveled vicariously through me. That's how my blog Pacnplay got started.

My co-workers encouraged me to start a blog about traveling. The blog eventually advanced to organizing trips for others. It's still hard for me to believe that I have traveled to 50 countries, mostly solo, and many of them I've repeated several times. These are places I used to read about in books and see in magazines and movies. I once traveled all the way to Bali and Rome because of the movie *Eat, Pray, Love* starring Julia Roberts. It was fascinating to visit the cities where the movie was filmed, and I learned so much about myself in these two beautiful countries.

I totally understand why some women are afraid to travel solo. I was once afraid as well. Women in general, and particularly black women, have many boundaries that society puts in place for us. I've learned in my lifetime that there are no boundaries or limitations in life, except the ones I place for myself. People ask me if I experienced racism while traveling outside of the United States. My answer is no. I have never experienced anyone being unkind to me in any way. So far, my experience has been nothing but welcoming. I know some women have experienced racism and I'm sorry they had that experience. I hope I never do.

I never let hearsay deter me from visiting a destination. I research for myself, then base my decision to visit on my findings with some regard to the experience of others, and most importantly, my own intuition.

## Preface

It's nice to look at and appreciate the travel photos of other people, but there's nothing better than visiting a place and creating your own memories. Solo travel has allowed me to love and understand myself on a deep and spiritual level. It's not just about the destination, but the journey and my time spent there. Solo travel may not be for everyone. However, I do suggest that everyone try it at least once. It doesn't have to be far. You can go domestically or travel internationally. Just go! This is why I wrote this book. I want to encourage you to travel solo. Step out of your comfort zone and try something new and different. I will share some of my solo travel experiences with you and some of my aha moments. I will provide you with information that will help you travel solo safely and well-informed. I'll give you tips on planning, budgets, safety, money exchange, packing, passport, visas, loneliness, and so much more.

Remember, this information is from my experience over the years, things I have learned from trial and error. Of course, each person's experience is their own. I don't make any guarantee that you won't make any errors or have mishaps. I'm an avid traveler, and I still run into hiccups every now and then. Now is the time for you to stop traveling vicariously through others and experience it for yourself. Live out your fantasies. Get to know your true self. You'd be surprised at the things that you will learn about yourself. Make that dream destination become a reality. It's time to Pacnplay. Let's go! You will not regret it.

# CHAPTER 1

# How It All Began

*"We travel not to escape life, but for life not to escape us."*
**Author unknown**

I've always been a dreamer and fascinated with travel. I don't know if I dreamed so much because I believed I could achieve my dreams or if it was a way to escape my reality. My life wasn't bad, it was just lonely at times. I was a latchkey child. This means I was home alone after school until my mother or older brother got there. I wasn't allowed to go outside or have company without my parents or brother being there. So, television, books, and my imagination became my best friends.

I would act out scenes as if I were producing a movie. I would write a script and I was profoundly serious about it. I had Barbie and Ken dolls. I would sneak my brother's GI Joe dolls in for a couple of scenes. The movies I would produce were usually in an exotic or tropical location, mostly Hawaii. I loved Elvis Presley's movie *Blue Hawaii*. I would dress my dolls up in different clothing and what I didn't have, I would make with paper and colored it with crayons. I grew up in the 70s, a time before computers and video games existed. This is how I started my love of travel and my destination list.

As a child, I traveled with my family and it was usually to South Carolina or New Jersey, except for the big family reunion, which happened every other year. At the end of the reunion, we would vote for where we want to have the next one. Florida was about the furthest and most tropical place we went. My mother and others were afraid to fly so that limited where we could go. Besides, some of the family members had lots of children, so we had to keep costs down or donate to help everyone be able to attend. Regardless of where we went, these were beautiful and fun times, filled with laughter, great memories, and of course, the occasional drama. You know when you get that many family members together, there will always be drama and secrets revealed. Be prepared for the drama at any family gathering, especially funerals and reunions. Those skeletons burst out of the closet. I'm laughing right now reminiscing about it.

Okay, I said all of this to say it takes lots of planning to organize group trips. How often have you planned or been part of a group or family vacation that never happened? As the deadlines grow near, the number of people participating usually decreases until the trip is cancelled or only one or two people go. That's how I went on my first solo international trip. A co-worker organized a trip to Aruba. I was so excited. This was in 1984. No passport was needed, just your birth certificate, a state ID or driver's license. Aruba is known as, "One Happy Island" located in the Caribbean, but belonging to the Netherlands. It was extremely popular among the elite back then, but it was still affordable at the time. It wasn't built up as it is today.

I was young, inexperienced, very insecure, and traveling out of the country for the first time without family or close friends. The group started with 12 people. Slowly, that group dwindled down to four people, and then eventually two, myself and an older co-worker that I barely knew. However, we decided we would make the best of it. I was so disappointed when she had a family emergency and had to cancel, so I was the last person standing. My dilemma was, if I didn't go, I would forfeit the entire cost of the trip. I didn't purchase travel insurance. I didn't know such a thing existed. (I will speak about travel insurance in a later chapter.)

So, off to Aruba I went. I didn't have a plan other than to go and enjoy myself. I was afraid, but the fear subsided very quickly. I just used the same safety survival skills I used at home in Brooklyn, New York. I only notified the hotel front desk that I was traveling alone, and they took great care of me. They monitored my comings and goings. I stayed at the resort most of the time. When I did venture out, it was on an excursion offered by the hotel, with a group. I watched my surroundings, and I was cautious of who I spoke to and the information I divulged.

Aruba was very safe then and still is now for everyone, including solo female travelers. I had a marvelous time. I met many people and was very welcomed in their circle. I have never regretted my decision to travel solo. Aruba became my favorite island for many years. I have revisited it several times, all on solo vacations, and I'm always amazed at its beauty and friendliness. It has the most beautiful beaches. I like the calmness of the Island. It's very relaxing and slow-paced.

I love traveling with friends and family. It's great making beautiful memories and spending time together. Group travel is amazing when everyone is on the same page. I had two wonderful friends that I loved to travel with, Laura and Wendy. I met them on a travel assignment in California. I became good friends with them, and we began to take girl trips. We traveled so well together. There was never a problem with anything. If challenges occurred, we handled them like adults and moved on. We shared some great times together. They were both younger than me and wanted to settle down and have a family of their own. They moved to different parts of the country to settle down and the group trips ceased. However, I'm still friends with both. I haven't traveled the same with anyone else.

I can tell you that I've seen more friendships end or become strained due to a vacation gone wrong. It has happened to me. Today, I'm still trying to figure out what went wrong. There was no argument or exchange of words. When we returned, she just stopped speaking to me or taking my calls. There's nothing like going on vacation and feeling like you hadn't just returned from one. Vacations are not cheap and taking time off work can be challenging for some. The more I travel solo, the more I love it and trips with other people are becoming less and less. I value my "me time". I like not being stressed and dealing with other people's drama or emotions while I'm on vacation. Solo travel allows me to just do me. I avoid all drama and stress unless I cause it.

# How It All Began

CHAPTER 2

# What's In It For Me?

*"Solo travel not only pushes you out of your comfort zone, but it also pushes you out of the zone of others' expectations."*
**Suzy Strutner**

Solo Traveling helps you peel back the interlayers of yourself. It engages you to discover who you are, but it also helps to reveal the person you've always been. On every one of my solo adventures, just like peeling an onion, a layer of my inner self is pulled back. Not only do I discover something new about myself, but I connect with a part of me that I had neglected or totally forgotten existed.

When I was in Rome, Italy, I reconnected with my love of opera and classical music. This wasn't my intention. When I

## What's In It For Me?

was planning my trip to Italy, I never thought about opera or classical music. It wasn't part of my itinerary at all. I was going to Rome to visit all the historical sites, eat Italian food and shop. Yes, I must admit, I also wanted to see if Italian men were as gorgeous and charming as portrayed in the movies. Ladies, the answer is yes and so much more. I was in a taxi going from my hotel to the Roman Coliseum. I was so full of excitement, who wouldn't be? I was minutes away from crossing an item off my bucket list that I had dreamed about for so many years. A building that was vastly enriched in history and amazing architectural design. It's over 1900 years old. The largest amphitheatre in the world, depicted in many movies and one of the new seven wonders of the world.

I couldn't help to think about all the events that took place there, the good, the bad, and the ugly. I tried to envision the stories that would be told if what was left of the standing walls could talk. My heart was pounding, and my hands were sweaty just trying to imagine, so I closed my eyes to relax my mind. Suddenly, I found myself drifting into another time and place. I was going back in time, but not the time of the Roman period, my time. Up until that point, I hadn't noticed the music. The driver was playing opera and I knew this song very well. It was a song from *La Boheme,* a very famous Italian opera by Giacomo Puccini. A beautiful but sad love story. The song was *Che Gelida Mania* by Luciano Pavarotti.

I found myself humming to it, getting lost in the music and delving into my childhood memories that were so entwined with this genre of music, savoring every note. My heartbeat slowed down and I felt calm, warm, and safe. A huge smile came across my face. For just a few minutes, I stepped back into my own history, remembering a period that was so meaningful and

## On My Own

fulfilling. Music has always been a huge part of my life. When I was in elementary school, I had the privilege to study music. I learned to play the trumpet, clarinet and oboe. I continued to play throughout junior high school and high school.

My junior high school instructor, Mr. Barry, was such a connoisseur of music. He taught us all categories of music, but opera and classical music were his favorites. The faces of enthusiasm he would make as he was instructing us. How he would nod and move his head to the beat of the music, always with a smile on his face, it was like he was in a trance. He would wave his baton with such force that I was afraid it would slip out of his hand and hit one of us. When the music really ignited him, he would jump up and down. His eyes would light up like a child's face on Christmas morning when we played well, or at least tried our best. But when we didn't, he looked like Mr. Scrooge.

Mr. Barry was a small-framed, black man in his early 50s. He was about five feet and six inches tall. He had a mustache that curled up at the ends and a full beard with sideburns. We used to tease him about his half-afro, which meant he was bald in the center of his head. I don't recall ever seeing him wear anything other than suits. Every day he wore a suit with a white shirt and a loud, colorful bow tie. Mr. Barry made music fun and very easy to learn. He didn't just teach us how to play the instruments, but he taught us the history of the instruments and the music he introduced to us. He felt that as children of color, it was very important for us to be exposed to experiences and things outside of what was considered the norm in our society. He used to say, "You may not understand it now, but you will appreciate it later." And yes, he was right.

## What's In It For Me?

I grew up in public housing in Brooklyn, New York. The dominant genres of music there were rap, gospel, R&B, reggae and a little jazz. If you played and listened to anything other than these, you were made fun of and criticized. Later in life, being eclectic in music and immersed in culture diversity opened many doors for me. Many of the doors have allowed me to meet people that I have built beautiful relationships with, the cab driver in Italy for instance. Salvatore and I became friends, and he became my personal driver for the duration of my visit to Rome.

It amazes me that just those few moments in that cab ride peeled back many layers of my inner self. It helped me remember that I loved opera, and I hadn't had the pleasure of listening to it in a long time. It also brought back precious memories of a person who has played a major role in my life. Mr. Barry opened my heart to different types of music and cultural experiences. He was the first person to teach me not to let society and other people dictate what to like and how to be. If I would have been in that cab with family or friends, I doubt that nostalgic moment would have occurred. I would probably have been too engaged in conversation with them to even have paid attention to the music playing. I might not have been open to talking to Salvatore.

Once I got home, I continued listening to opera and classical music. I still smile and get that warm feeling. I even think about taking music lessons to play the clarinet again. How about you? Have you ever had a moment like that, a moment where you were alone and something triggered a pleasant memory for you, something you had completely forgotten about? If so, how did it make you feel?

## On My Own

So often, we as women become wrapped up in the pleasures of our loved ones, it's easy to forget what we like or what we don't get to experience often. When you have small children, they often take over everything. It doesn't matter how many televisions are in the house. They want to watch the one you're watching. Then they hold you prisoner because they don't want to be alone. So instead of watching your favorite program or something you're generally interested in, you're stuck watching reruns of the same cartoon or movie for the thousandth time. You've memorized every scene and every song. I can still sing all the *Barney,* the purple dinosaur, songs. I also remember every scene and every song from the movie *Little Shop of Horrors.*

As women, we're naturally nurturers. We please others all the time, often neglecting ourselves and our feelings. Sometimes, we're afraid or don't like being alone, so we end up doing things or going to places we really don't want to. Have you ever gone on a vacation with family or friends, and you hardly got to do anything you wanted to do? Most of the group wanted to do something else. You went along with the plan to keep the peace, or because you didn't want to do your activity alone. When you travel solo, you can plan the trip to cater to you totally. If you change your mind, it's okay. You're not inconveniencing anyone but yourself. I have canceled and changed the dates and times of many excursions. Sometimes, I wake up and don't feel like doing what I have planned, so I don't. It's that simple. No drama.

Traveling solo also allows you to sleep in late or get up early. You can sleep with the television on, listen to music or sleep in silence. You can walk around in the nude and keep the room cold or hot. You can be as neat or as messy as you like. You can be as active or lazy as you want. One of my trips to Puerto Rico is a perfect example of this. I love Hispanic food. I love the flavors of Puerto Rican and Cuban cuisine. While living in New York, there was no shortage of any type of ethnic food besides restaurants, I also had many friends that would keep me stuffed with their traditional dishes.

When I moved to South Carolina, the only Spanish restaurants I could find were Mexican. I like it, but it's not my favorite. I began to travel for food. Once I took a cruise with my best friend and we found this little mom-and-pop restaurant in San Juan, a local person told us about it. It's a restaurant that the locals go to eat on their lunch break and dinner with their families. We had been shopping and wanted to eat before going back on board the ship. It wasn't on the main strip where all the tourists and overpriced restaurants were. It was located on a side street, several blocks from the main street. I can't give you directions, however, I can take you right to it. It has the best Puerto Rican food I've ever tasted. The restaurant feels like you're sitting in someone's home surrounded by family and friends, such a warm feeling.

The customer service is great too. My favorite dish there is the fried snapper, rice and peas, sweet fried plantains, and a side salad. I can smell and taste it right now. One day, I was craving Puerto Rican food and memories of that restaurant crossed my mind. I decided to fly to Puerto Rico for five days to eat, relax, and shop. I was married at the time, working as an emergency room nurse and just needed some *"me time"* away from the job, husband and kids.

I went to the restaurant as soon as I arrived, but for the next few days, I didn't leave the property of the hotel. I just laid on the beach, read my book, and enjoyed pleasant conversations with people I met. It wasn't until the fourth day that I started to explore the beautiful island. That's the best thing about solo travel, you can do anything or nothing at all. If I would have been with someone, I might not have been able to do that so easily. I returned home a well-rested woman, mentally and physically ready to give my family and my patients at the hospital what they needed from me.

I know some of you are thinking you don't have the time or money to travel. You don't have to venture far. You don't have to spend a fortune. You can travel on any budget. Research is the key, and I'll talk more about it later. I'm an avid solo traveler. I will find any excuse to travel somewhere. I will travel to shop and oh my goodness, overnight or day trips are the best for shopping. I don't know too many women that don't love retail therapy. Taking an early morning drive out of your town or state to your favorite outlet or shopping mall is so relaxing. I love to drive alone. It's therapy for me. It helps me clear my thoughts. I'll play my favorite music or just drive in silence and have conversations with God or even myself.

Sometimes you must work things out within yourself and *"me time"* is very rewarding. Once I arrive, I can take my time and shop. There's no one there to give an opinion that I didn't ask for on what I buy or how much I spend on it. I get to go to the stores I like or just explore. Later, I'll treat myself to a nice meal, go back to my hotel room and relax. Taking a bath or shower with no interruptions is therapeutic all by itself. It also gives me time to go through my purchases to decide if I want to return anything before, I leave. I've traveled solo to conferences, sporting events, the theatre and concerts. I love reggae music and will travel far to see my two favorite artists, Kymani Marley and Beres Hammond.

## What's In It For Me?

Buying a single ticket is so much easier than buying multiple. You have better seat choices and it's easier to go backstage to meet the artist and take a photo after the concert if you're alone versus with someone else or a group.

There's a famous quote that says, *"If something good happens, travel to celebrate. If something bad happens, travel to forget. If nothing happens, travel to make something happen."* Solo travel always allows you to be your true, authentic self, and you can live out your fantasies and dreams. There's no one there to judge or try to talk you out of it.

I was a flamenco dancer in Spain. I've had photo shoots as a queen in Thailand, Turkey, and Egypt. I was even an honorary flight attendant on Emirates Airline on my way home from Dubai. I danced on the bar in Jamaica. Now you talk about fun. My list goes on and on. These are memories that I will forever cherish. Yes, I have done some crazy and adventurous things traveling with friends and family, but it was always more fun and memorable on my solo trips because I did it for me, not because of someone else. No one coerced me to do it, I did it because I wanted to do it, and it brought me pleasure. That's part of self-love, learning how to do the things that are meaningful to you without guilt or shame. Solo travel will teach you brand-new skills and enhance the ones you already have. Let's talk about it in the next chapter.

# On My Own

## What's In It For Me?

CHAPTER 3

# Learning From My Journey

*"A journey takes time and the lessons we learn best, they come from the journey, not the destination."*
**Jordan Dane**

Solo travel has taught me to enjoy and learn from the journey as well as the destination. I've completely changed the way I view and understand the world and where I fit in it. My life skills have also been enhanced. I'm speaking about everyday survival skills. I'm no longer living with self-doubt, lack of confidence, and walking in fear. I no longer allow other people's self-limiting beliefs and negativity to spill over into my subconscious mind, preventing me from doing things I desire. Today I hold myself in high regard. I'm confident and I have learned how to work through my fears. I'm pursuing and achieving goals and dreams that I've put off for far too long. I'm truly in love with myself and caring for myself on a deep and spiritual level. What a wonderful feeling! I'm finally the CEO of my life and loving it! Solo travel has helped me with:

## CONFIDENCE

Traveling solo can be scary in the beginning. The more trips I went on by myself, the more confident I became, and the feelings of uncertainty became less and less. Solo travel teaches you just how capable you are at taking care of yourself. I remember when I sat down in my seat on the plane for my first solo trip. I said, "Wow, I'm really doing this." My confidence level was boosted, and the fear started to subside.

## TRUST

I have learned how to trust myself and decide who I should trust. It's this thing called intuition or gut feeling. A lot of women ignore it. It's very important for your safety and protection to listen to your gut. If it doesn't feel right, then it's probably not right. However, you can't keep your guard completely up all the time. You're going to have to trust some people at some point. We do it all the time at home without thinking about it. We go to a restaurant, and we trust total strangers to prepare the food we eat. We sit down in a chair without thinking and trust that it will bear our weight. We get in a taxi and trust the driver will take us where we've asked to go. The key is to stay alert, watch your surroundings, and gather information to quickly make an informed decision on what to do.

## BUDGETING

Traveling solo has helped me learn how to handle finances better. I've learned how to save and pay close attention to my bills. I'm better at stretching a dollar. I try to pay off debt quickly. When you travel solo there's no one else in your immediate area to fall back on if a financial crisis occurs. So, you must be prepared for incidentals.

## INDEPENDENCE

I've always considered myself to be independent. I'm part of Generation X. I grew up as a latchkey child in New York City. I had to take care of myself until my mother came home from work. I was forced to be alone a lot and eventually grew to love it. Solo travel just deepened my knowledge of what being independent means. I became better with my finances. I try to take care of my mental, spiritual and physical health. I'm in tune with myself. If you aren't already independent, solo travel will help you get there. You're on your own and the only person you can depend on for sure is you.

## DECISION MAKING

I'm great with decision-making at my job and with my clients. When it came to my personal life, I used to be the master of indecisiveness. It was mostly out of fear. I wasn't sure if I was doing the right thing. Besides, I'm a Gemini and I'm back and forth with everything. I'll decide and moments later, I may change my mind and go back to the previous decision. Since traveling solo, I'm better at making decisions without second-guessing.

The great thing about solo travel is the decisions you make only affect you. You don't have to feel guilty or ashamed.

## PROBLEM-SOLVING

As a nurse administrator and life coach, I'm very good at problem-solving. I solve other people's problems all day. Solo travel has enhanced it. There are problems that can occur during your travel that you will need to solve. You must think quickly on your feet. Travel delays, missed flights, lost luggage, problems with your phone. The hotel may not look like the pictures. You can't find your transportation to your accommodation. The list can go on and on. Some things may have been caused by you and some are simply out of your control. The great news is you're capable of solving these issues and you will figure it out. The key is not to panic. Take a deep breath and think about how you're going to respond. You may not have control of the event, but you're in complete control of how you respond and that will greatly influence the outcome.

## POSITIVE ATTITUDE

During my travels, I've learned how spoiled we are as Americans. Immediate gratification is a big part of the American culture. Other cultures don't move as quickly or share the same customs. Things that we do here may be done differently somewhere else. It doesn't make it wrong, it's just their way of doing it. In many European countries, they have siesta time. The local shops and restaurants close in the middle of the day and reopen later in the evening. They use this time to relax, take a nap, or spend time with their family. I've seen Americans throw a fit and become very rude because restaurants were closed. It was an inconvenience for them, and they were not happy. In Italy, it's customary not to rush. Europeans love to sit and relax before ordering. They take time to eat and enjoy their meal. Eating is very social. It's a time to spend with family and friends, not just for nourishing your body. The waiter may take a long time to bring your check. They're not slow or ignoring you, it's just the custom. If you're on a tight schedule, just tell the server before you place your order.

I had to learn this quickly. I'm from New York City, it's very fast-paced there. Everyone is always looking at a clock or their watch, rush, rush, rush! I've learned to keep a positive attitude. I also study the customs of the country I'm visiting prior to my trip. This way, I know what to expect. I plan accordingly and adjust to the culture.

## TAPPING INTO MY DIVINE FEMININE ENERGY

The word feminine means having qualities, or an appearance, traditionally associated with women. The energy of the feminine encompasses softness but can be fierce when necessary. (Think of when someone hurts a mother's baby.) Feminine energy is nurturing, compassionate, healing, intuitive, sensual, magnetic, receptive, confident, and relaxed in just being. It's fluid like the ocean. It's the total opposite of masculine energy, which is about needing to be busy most of the time. Masculine energy is assertive, logical, loves to problem solve, goal-driven, giving and very decisive.

Feminine and masculine energy exists in all things and people. Despite gender, everyone has both masculine and feminine energy. One cannot exist without the other. It's like yin and yang, they complement each other. They're equally important. However, we must learn to balance these two energies in order to live in harmony with our mind, body, and spirit. Too much or too little of either can cause dysfunction in your life. On your self-love journey, it's very important to tap into your feminine energy. Your feminine energy is what allows you to relax, slow down and recharge to be at your best. Feminine energy allows you to connect deeply with yourself. It helps you to love and trust yourself. As you start to feel the love and build trust in yourself, you will begin to have a high regard for yourself. This will empower you to relinquish self-doubt, fear and feelings of inadequacy.

Feminine energy allows you to just be present in the moment and go with the flow of life. Without feminine energy, you rest in masculine energy, a state of constantly doing, striving to achieve more, being competitive, and getting things done. It's great to work towards and achieve goals, but you don't want to stay in this type of energy all the time. It will exhaust you. It can eventually lead to physical or emotional illness. Everyone, regardless of gender, must take time to relax and recharge. At home, I used to rest in my masculine energy too often, always going and doing for others, always giving. I had a hard time receiving. I felt very shy or embarrassed if anyone tried to give me gifts. I hardly ever put myself first. If it wasn't my children, it was my husband, my work and then my aging parents. When I finally slowed down, I was too tired to do anything. All I wanted to do was sleep. Solo travel has allowed me to rest in my feminine, to just be. I'm not on anyone's clock. I can do the things that make me happy without compromising or feeling guilty.

## On My Own

When I was in Rome, I met a man. I was having lunch outside of a restaurant near the Spanish Steps. He walked right up to me and started talking and asked if he could sit with me. I didn't look up at him because I really didn't want to be bothered. I was at peace and truly didn't want to be disturbed. The truth is, I went through a bad and bitter divorce a few years earlier and didn't trust men. I didn't care how nice or good-looking they were. I was in my hate-men phase. He really didn't give me a chance to say no. He pulled the chair out and sat down. At first, I glanced around to see if all the other seats were occupied. There were plenty of empty seats. Then I looked up and I could care less about anything going on around me. This man was gorgeous! Mid 40's, 5'10, medium build, olive skin, dark brown, wavy hair with soft green eyes that melted my heart and took away all my defenses. He was wearing khaki, loose-fitting pants with a fitted white tee shirt and sandals.

I got so nervous that I knocked over my water glass. It went all over the table and trickled down my white cotton skirt. He quickly came to my rescue and cleaned the table while I tried to get myself together. When the waiter came to assist to clean the table, he immediately shifted his attention to me and helped me dry my skirt with a table napkin. I was so embarrassed. He was kneeling, helping me and I couldn't look up at him. I kept apologizing and he kept assuring me that everything was okay. Then he took his fingers on his right hand and placed them gently under my chin. He preceded to lift my chin upwards so that I was forced to look at those beautiful green eyes. Then he softly said in a very thick Italian accent, "It's okay, you're okay, I'm okay, we are okay. Now relax." I melted like butter in a hot saucepan and all my senses were in overdrive.

## Learning From My Journey

We will call my friend Fabio. He said he had been watching me the day before at the Spanish steps taking pictures with my tripod. He was intrigued by how I was so focused on taking photos of myself. I looked like I was in a world all alone enjoying my time. He thought that I was a very beautiful and unique woman full of confidence and mystery. He also stated he loved my curves, as he gestured my shape with his hands. At the time, I was a size 16. He stated he was too afraid to speak to me then but hoped I would return the next day and he would have the courage to approach me. When he saw me again and saw that I was still alone, he decided to go for it.

The Spanish steps is a famous place in Rome where people come together to chill out and people-watch. It's busy during the day but really comes alive at night with parties and music. People get married there and take wedding photos. It has approximately 175 stairs with Trinita' dei Monti church at the top and Piazza di Spagna at the base with a water fountain called Fontana della Barcaccia (Fountain of the Old Boat).

Fabio and I ate lunch together. We talked about so many things. His English was very good, and he enjoyed my broken Italian. After lunch we walked, and he was my private tour guide. I must admit I thought he was a gigolo at first. Turns out, he was an architect in Rome on business. He lives in Verona. Fabio was such a gentleman. He held my hand. Always made sure I was on the inside of the curb. He would gently place his hand on my waist to help guide me in and out of the crowds. He kept feeding me all types of Italian pastries and different flavors of gelato.

The best thing was he loves to shop. He would not allow me to pay for anything. He said he just wanted me to enjoy Italy and keep a smile on my face so he could see my dimples. My feet started to hurt from all the walking we did. We were in a park called Villa Borghese. It has a museum with a beautiful landscape. He carried me on his back to a bench, sat me down and rubbed my feet while he sang Italian. For the next two days, I was treated like a queen, but he made me feel like a princess. I didn't want my time with him to end, but Morocco was my next and last destination before the long journey home. He was headed home the day after my departure. He asked me to travel with him.

Fabio made me remember what it's like to be a sensuous woman. I remembered what it feels like when a man cares about you. How they treat you. How they go out of their way to ensure your safety, comfort and happiness. He brought my softness out. I was just enjoying every moment, going with the flow, something I had not done in a long time. I was completely able to rest in my feminine and enjoyed being on the receiving end of things. He made every decision on what we would do and where we should go. He even ordered my food, but it wasn't in a controlling way. He would say, "Darling try it. If you don't like, we'll order something else." Then he would kiss me on my forehead and the top of my hand. He was just very gentle and kind to me, so I had no problem allowing him to take the lead.

I learned that my experience with my ex-husband should not be placed on every man's shoulder. It's not their weight to carry. Sometimes, relationships don't last or work out for numerous reasons. It's not the end of life. Give yourself time to heal so you don't bring baggage from a past relationship into a new one. Then open your heart again to the chance of new love and friendships. Fabio raised the bar, so now I have raised my standards when it comes to dating and men. I know my worth and won't settle for less than I deserve.

What ever happened to me and Fabio? We kept in touch briefly. He came into my life for a reason and his purpose was fulfilled. He vanished as quickly as he entered. I have no regrets. I'll always remember him and what significance he played in my life. Maybe I'll share more details about us in another book. A romance novel. Would you like that?

# On My Own

CHAPTER 4

# Loneliness And Solo-friendly Destinations

*"Traveling solo does not always mean you're alone. Most often, you meet marvelous people along the way and make connections that last a lifetime."*
**Jacqueline Boone**

The question I get asked most frequently about solo travel is, "Do you ever get lonely?" My answer is, "Very rarely." Solo travel is not for everyone, at least not on a consistent basis. You must really like spending time with yourself. I suggest that you take small steps, getting comfortable being on your own. Start with going out to eat alone, then progress to going to the movies, and eventually a short weekend getaway. I've been traveling solo

## On My Own

for years and the more time I spend alone, the more I love it. I started to feel guilty about it. I had to teach myself that it was okay to enjoy my own company.

Traveling solo has given me the ability to reinvent myself into the person I am today, a person that I'm totally proud of. I've become a very strong, confident, outgoing, and loving person of myself and others. I've learned to rely solely on myself. I've gained assurance of my judgment and instincts. I've also met some amazing people that have become part of my family. If I had traveled with a group, I might not have been open to talking or interacting with them.

People are very receptive to solo travelers, and I found them to be very protective as well. I took a boat tour in Phuket, Thailand. I met a Chinese family that was visiting from Bali, Indonesia. I fell in love with the grandmother. She spoke no English, but she would just motion to me with her hands and smile. She was so adorable. For some reason, she and I were drawn to each other. She introduced me to her entire family and from that moment, I wasn't alone. That family accepted me into their circle. They included me in everything they did. It was raining on the way back and the water was very rough on the boat.

Many people got motion sickness, including me. My new family huddled around me and took care of me. They made sure I got on the bus that would take me back to my hotel. They made me promise to notify them that I arrived safely. I learned during our time together that the eldest son and I shared the same birthday in the same year. He's only hours older than me. We were both in Thailand and celebrating our birthdays. I now have a Chinese twin brother, lol! The two of us remind me of Arnold Schwarzenegger and Danny Devito in the movie, "Twins." He's only 4'10 and I'm 5'9. We manage to stay in contact.

## Loneliness And Solo-friendly Destinations

There are many things you can do to avoid feeling lonely…

When planning your vacation, choose your accommodations wisely. Until you become accustomed to solo travel. Stay in a hotel with lots of amenities that's not isolated. Try a location in a city or a large town. This way, you can walk around, familiarize yourself with the area and get to socialize with the locals. They can give you pointers on where to go and what to do. The hotel front desk or concierge can be helpful too. You can enjoy the spa and have conversations there with the attendants or other guests. You can also go to the lounge and get involved in activities or enjoy whatever entertainment that's provided. There's also the pool and the pool bar. One of my favorite things to do is to sit and people-watch. I'm sure you will strike up a conversation with someone, or they will with you.

Group day tours are the best of both worlds. You're still solo, but you're not alone. It will help you to learn how to talk to strangers if you're an introverted person. Social butterflies like me will be in heaven. You'd be surprised at the diversity of people on these tours. People travel from all around the globe to go on vacation. It's a big world, but small at the same time. In Mexico, I met a lady that lived in the same city as me. She was also traveling solo. That was a cool experience. We hung out and we were each other's photographers the entire day. I never saw her again after that, but I still have those memories.

Sign up to take a class. Learning something new is a good way to be social. Usually, it commands participation as a group, I love learning new things. I love taking cooking classes to learn how to prepare some of the local dishes. Arts and crafts are another thing I enjoy. There are also classes and excursions that are organized for solo travelers to encourage engagement. I went on one in Madrid, Spain to a nightclub. I was afraid to go out alone. The concierge at my hotel told me about this night tour. We went to dinner, toured the city at night and then went to a nightclub. Transportation was included. I was picked up from and dropped back to the hotel and there was a guy that stayed with the group. He even danced with all the ladies. It was a great time on a Monday night.

A solo retreat is another way of traveling solo, but not being alone. Retreats are very intentional getaways. They're powerful, have long-term benefits, provide a safe sanctuary and allow you to get away from the daily stresses of life. You will be surrounded by like-minded people. And usually, you'll make long-lasting friendships. There are so many types to choose from, spa retreats, spiritual retreats, and health and wellness retreats. You can find them domestically or internationally. Some retreats can be less expensive than a vacation or some may be more depending on what they offer. The great thing is retreats don't require much planning.

Bring entertainment with you. I download my favorite movies to my iPad or laptop. I also take a good book or buy one at the airport. Another must-have is a journal. I write my everyday travel experiences in it, so I don't forget what I did. Sometimes you don't remember where a picture was taken or why you took it or the name of a restaurant you really enjoyed. Journaling is good when you can't sleep, or you wake up in the middle of the night and there's nothing to do. Just write about your adventures of the day.

Visit local cafes and restaurants away from the touristy areas. It doesn't have to be far away. Sometimes if you just take a turn down a side street, right off the main road, you'll find amazing places where the locals hang out, and get the scoop on what's happening in their town or city. There may be a concert or festival you didn't know about.

In Seville, Spain, I stumbled upon the cutest tapas bar around the corner from my hotel. A tapas bar is where you hang out with the locals. They serve a variety of Spanish appetizers, beer and wine. There's usually live entertainment. This bar had Flamenco dancing and I love Flamenco dancing. I had such a great time that I went back several nights.

The main thing with not getting that lonely feeling is to step out of your comfort zone. Try new things and be open but cautious. Traveling to unknown places and destinations will challenge you to be more open. There are times when you will need help and must ask for it. I remember getting so turned around in Venice, Italy for the first two days. All the piazzas (neighborhoods) looked the same. I ended up in the same one four times trying to get back to my hotel. Finally, I asked a local for assistance and she helped me with no problem. Speaking Italian was another task, but we will discuss language in another chapter.

*"You will never be alone if you like the person you're with."*

There are many destinations that are solo travel friendly for women. You can look up solo-friendly travel destinations online and you will see many variations because it's mostly subjective. People have different experiences, and they base their opinion on their experiences.

For example, Barcelona and Madrid in Spain are listed as solo-friendly. However, I didn't think they were as solo-friendly as other countries or cities I had visited. I enjoyed my time, but I was on guard so much because pickpocketing is a thing there. You must be extra careful not to stick out like a sore thumb. After two days, I had enough, I hired a private guide to travel with me everywhere in Barcelona. Once I hired a tour guide, I really enjoyed my time there. I was only in Madrid for two days and that was more than enough for me. In Seville and Granada, Spain it was totally different. I walked alone everywhere. My hotel was in a residential neighborhood. No one bothered me at all. I was still careful because pickpockets exist there too, but not to the extreme of Barcelona and Madrid. The locals were very friendly and very helpful. In fact, I'm planning a return trip to Seville. I remind you this was my experience. Other people may have had a different encounter. I hope you get the point.

The places I have travelled to that I felt the most comfortable as a solo traveler are Bali, Indonesia; Lisbon, Portugal; Seville, Spain; Phuket, Thailand; Reykjavik, Iceland; Amsterdam, Netherlands; London, England, Venice, Italy; Cartagena, Colombia; Negril, Jamaica, and all of Cuba, Aruba, Bahamas, St. Maarten, Turks and Caicos, St. Lucia, Maldives and the list keeps growing.

The best advice I can give to you is not to let anyone sway you from traveling to a destination based solely on their experience. Everyone's encounter is their own. Always do your own research. Then base your decision on that. I will talk about research in another chapter.

*"If you never go, you will never know."*

## Loneliness And Solo-friendly Destinations

CHAPTER 5

# Where Do I Start?

*"20 years from now, you will be more disappointed by the things you didn't do than by the things you did do."*
**Mark Twain**

The hardest part of solo traveling is getting started. Deciding to actually go is a very courageous endeavor. Emotions of fear and doubt will find you all through your planning stage. You may have thoughts like, "Am I crazy?", "Can I really do this?", "Should I do this?". Just take a deep breath and remind yourself of the reason you wanted to go solo in the first place. That will usually motivate you to continue with your plans.

Before I get into the how-to-plan chapter, we need to talk about purpose and experience. What's the reason you want to travel at this time? What type of experience are you looking for? Answering these two questions will help you choose your destination, type of accommodations, itinerary and budget much easier. Think of places you've always wanted to go, and why you want to visit them, write them down. Try and narrow it down to your top three, basing your decision on your current state of being. Are you depressed and need to get away? Are you bored and need some excitement or an adventure? Are you overworked and stressed and just need some downtime? Are you celebrating something? Whatever you do, don't get caught up in fad traveling. Don't go visit a place because everyone else is going, unless you have a personal purpose and experience expectation. If not, the destination will probably not fulfill your expectations, and your trip will not be successful. It will be money and time wasted.

My trip to Bali, Indonesia is a perfect example. My focus for that trip was spirituality. I went there to connect with my God and myself. It was a spiritual journey. My father had been diagnosed with prostate cancer and I was his sole caregiver. I was angry and I was tired. I was working two jobs, and I was in school full-time working on my next degree. I felt lost and I was confused as his daughter, but I was very frustrated as a registered nurse. It's hard watching someone you love slowly die in front of you. People don't realize how difficult it is to take care of someone 24 hours a day. You get all caught up in their emotions and you become numb. You don't have any of your own or you can't take the time to recognize or express them because you're too busy caring for your loved ones every need. Thanks to respite care, an organization that provides short-term relief for primary caregivers. They came into the home and stayed with my father 24 hours a day, allowing me to take the much-needed vacation.

## On My Own

I flew to Bali, and I went to multiple temples. I participated in cleansing ceremonies. I did yoga and meditation every day. Even though Bali has some of the most beautiful beaches, that wasn't my primary reason for the trip. But the last two days out of the nine, I did spend time at the beach. I hired a driver and spent time at several beaches all around Bali. It was the perfect relaxation and preparation for the long flight home. When I returned home, I was a much better me and I was able to care for my father until his dying day. Today, I have no regrets about the time I spent with him, how tired I was, how hard it was. My father died with his dignity and in his home that he cherished so much.

Now, Jamaica is one of the loves of my life. I have been to Jamaica so many times that I've stopped counting stamps in my passport. When I go to Jamaica, it's not about the big hotels and all the amenities. Of course, when I first started traveling there, I did all the touristy things. I stayed at luxury resorts. Now, I go to Jamaica simply to relax and get my thoughts together. I become a beach bum every day, just listening to music, people watching and getting some writing done. I just zone in on the culture and I'm very comfortable in Jamaica. So, my accommodations are very minimal. I don't expect much. I stay at little family-run hotels on the beach in Negril or Ocho Rios. The food is home cooked. The rooms are not fancy, but very clean with that home feeling and the customer service is out of this world. My purpose and experience expectations were completely different for each of these locations, allowing me to thoroughly enjoy myself.

When I went to Egypt, my purpose was to continue finding myself, but I also had a point to prove to myself. I always felt connected to Africa, but Egypt in particular. I was on a self-love journey. My goal was to visit as many African countries as possible. I started with Egypt because of all the documented history. I was always fascinated with the place. It was also my dream trip for a very long time.

My plan was to visit as many historical sites as possible. I had a desire to visit museums, temples, and cruise down the Nile River. I wanted to buy jewelry, Egyptian cotton, sheets, spices, oils, etc. I knew I needed to stay in a very nice hotel and to have a travel guide to escort me around. I also understood my budget had to be big for me to really enjoy myself, so I saved immensely for this trip. I gathered as much information from reading books, watching movies, and YouTube. I also spoke to people who have visited there already. When I went to Egypt, I had the time of my life. Without purpose and experience expectation, I might not have enjoyed it as much. I do know several people who have gone to Egypt and didn't like it.

When I was in high school, I admired my gym teacher. She was an older African American woman who traveled all the time. She had taken a trip to Egypt over the spring break and was telling the students about it. I expressed to her I wanted to be like her and travel to Egypt and many other countries. It was then she looked at me and said, "Unfortunately, you will have a lot of babies and go nowhere."

I was frozen. I looked at her with disbelief. Did she really just say that to me and mean it? What did she see in me that would make her say that? Did she see me on a path of destruction? That word "unfortunately" stuck with me for a long time. I didn't allow it to kill my spirit, but it became a fire that blazed deep in my spirit. A fire of determination to get out of the projects of Brooklyn and live a life of purpose and fulfillment. I had some mishaps along the way, who doesn't? I moved my family out of the projects in 1996. I finally made it to Egypt in 2018 at the age of 52, a proud professional with three college degrees. I had traveled to 26 countries by then, some of them many times. I had been to Jamaica over 30 times.

The one thing she was correct about was me having many children. I have given birth to two beautiful children and adopted many along the way. They call me "Mama Sandra" because of the respect, love and admiration they have for me. It brings joy to my heart every time I hear one of them call me Mama Sandra. I've been a positive influential force in their lives and them in mine. Together, we've learned many life lessons. The one thing I have never told any of them is what they could not become or do. I've always encouraged them to be their best, dream big and pursue these dreams. Most importantly, anything is possible if you put forward the effort and believe in yourself.

I love the story of Pharaoh Ramses II and his favorite wife Queen Nefertari. To see this beautiful monument in person was amazing. What you cannot see are the tears of joy streaming down my face. I'm saying quietly to myself repeatedly, "I made it, I'm here, I never gave up on my dream and now I'm living it".

I've learned on my self-love journey, and now teach my clients, how to stop letting other people write your life story. You're the author of your story, and you determine how it ends. When you give others the pen, you relinquish your power. Take your power back and write a story that you desire and are so worthy of. Chapter by chapter. If don't like a chapter rewrite it, then go live it!

## Where Do I Start?

CHAPTER 6

# Planning Is Definitely A Process

*"The journey of a thousand miles begins with a single step."*
**Lao-Tzu**

The most important phase of planning is research. It's also the most time-consuming. I've learned if you research extensively, you will save yourself from losing money and time. Most importantly, you will be less likely to jeopardize your safety. Let's start planning step by step.

## WEATHER

After you have chosen your destination, research the weather for the time of year you want to travel. You don't want to go to a tropical island in rainy or monsoon season. You can't ski if there's no snow.

When I went to Phuket, Thailand in June, which starts the rainy season, it was the low season and inexpensive. I'll talk more about seasons later in this chapter. It rained every day, but not all day. However, the excursion I was looking forward to the most wasn't as great because of the weather. We couldn't stop at particular islands because of the rough water conditions. If the weather is suitable for you, then great. If not, choose another destination or time of year to visit.

## PASSPORT

Review what travel documents are required to travel to your chosen destination. Make sure your passport has at least six months before expiring from the return date of your travel. If not, you should apply immediately for a renewal. Most countries require that your passport has at least six months open. If you don't have a passport, I suggest you apply right away and wait until you receive it before you book your travel. You want to allow yourself room for error and delays. If you don't want to wait, then at least pay to have the application expedited. There's a space where you write in your travel date. You can receive your passport within a two-week timeframe if you expedite the process. Remember, this is an additional cost.

## VISA AND TRAVEL ALERTS

Research if there's a travel visa requirement. A travel visa is an official document that gives you permission to legally enter a foreign country for a predetermined time, usually between 30 or 90 days, and only as a tourist or leisure stay. As a US citizen, there are many countries you will not need a visa for, but there are some destinations that you must apply for a visa in advance. India is one that I know of. There are many destinations where you can obtain your visa on arrival. Visit **www.travel.state.gov**. This is the website for the US Department of State Bureau of Consular Affairs to check for visa requirements for US citizens to enter any country. You can also check the safety advisories for any country on this website as well.

Pay attention to the travel alerts. The alerts are not always about terrorists. Some alerts may indicate a country not being accepting of the LGBT community or there's a noted sex trafficking, kidnapping, harsh punishment for sex outside of marriage, etc. So read the alerts; you don't want to go somewhere that's not considered safe or has practices against your morals. The other website I use to check visa requirements is **www.cibtvisas.com**. A visa is an additional cost and prices vary per country.

## VACCINES FOR TRAVEL

Vaccination is a very controversial subject today. I'm not here to speak for or against vaccines. I'm going to provide you with details of where you can obtain the necessary information. The decision is yours to make. Certain countries suggest vaccinations for certain diseases, and then there are those that have made certain vaccinations mandatory. Depending on where you travel, you may come into contact with diseases that are rare In the United States. Yellow fever is one of those diseases. Brazil and certain countries in Africa have made this vaccine mandatory due to the high rates of reported cases.

The Center for Disease Control and Prevention (CDC) has a website, **www.cdc.gov** that you can visit and obtain all the information you need on vaccines for traveling abroad. Also, the US Department of State has another website, **https://travel.state.gov.com**.

Covid travel restrictions are constantly changing, even though many countries have lifted pre-Covid testing and vaccination verification, there are many that have restrictions in place. Be sure to know your destination's Covid-19 travel requirements. Each country has its own testing requirements. Some can be quite complicated; some destinations are still requiring quarantine. Be sure to know what your destination's quarantine protocol is. If you, unfortunately, get sick, you need to have a plan. Not all countries provide quarantine accommodations. Therefore, Covid-19 insurance is very important. (I'll talk more about insurance later).

You can check the embassy website for the country you're planning to visit for the most up-to-date information on Covid-19 and requirements for entry and departure from any country, including the United States. If you're a US citizen, you can check with the Center for Disease Control and Prevention. Also, the US Department of State Bureau of Consular Affairs, **https://travel.state.gov.com**.

These websites give you the country's Covid-19 status. They're coded by color for the level of risk of becoming ill from Covid.

Green is low risk. Yellow is median risk. Orange is high risk of getting sick. If flying, check Covid-19 testing requirements for the airline you plan to fly with. They may require testing when traveling internationally. If you have a layover in a different country than your destination, you should check their requirements as well. If your flight is delayed, you want to assure that if Covid testing is needed, you get tested prior to leaving home at the latest date possible. This will allot you time for mishaps like travel delays. If your Covid test expires on route, you will have to get tested prior to entry or even denied entry. If you plan on taking a cruise, you must check with the individual cruise line about Covid-19 travel requirements.

## BUDGET

How much money you can afford to spend is a key factor in vacation planning. There are times I had to change my destination because it didn't fit my travel budget. As a solo traveler, you must remember you're responsible for the entire trip. There's no one to fall back on, no one to split costs with, nobody's credit card to use or borrow money from if you come up short. You alone are the plan A, B, and C. Your budget should include flights, luggage, accommodations, visa, transportation to and from your hotel, excursions, entertainment, food and drinks, tips, a single supplement if there's one, and shopping. Include extra for incidentals. Most importantly, don't forget travel insurance. Treat yourself nicely but remember you must return home and continue to pay your living expenses.

When I went to Cuba, I had to take extra cash. The United States and Cuba are financially disconnected. Your credit cards issued from a United States Bank will not work in Cuba. You can bring US dollars and exchange them for Cuban pesos at certain banks, airports or informal markets. The fee for the exchange is very high. You cannot use US dollars in any Cuban government-owned facility. The Euro was the best currency to bring to Cuba when I went. It was widely accepted, and the island has the lowest bank fee when exchanging them. You can also exchange the Canadian dollar, the Swiss Franc, the pound sterling, and the Mexican peso. I exchanged US dollars for euros before I arrived in Cuba and what I did not spend, I exchanged to the US dollar once I arrived back in the United States.

# FLIGHTS

There are several booking sites to use to research flights and hotels. Always browse using incognito mode. The websites won't remember you and the prices will not increase, causing you to buy a ticket or make a hotel reservation in haste in fear of the price going up again. When researching flights, keep in mind the closest airport to you may not be the cheapest, even if it's an international airport. You may come out cheaper by flying from a different location. It's usually less expensive for me to book a domestic flight from Charlotte, North Carolina to New York City, then book my international flight to leave from New York City. The savings is usually hundreds of dollars for me. You can also drive to another airport if the cost is less. Factoring gas, parking and your time to ensure you're saving money and not losing it. You might decide the drive is not worth it and pay for the convenience of leaving from your city. When I went to Cartagena, Colombia, it was very expensive to fly out of Charlotte, North Carolina, so I booked a ticket from Orlando to Cartagena, nonstop. Drove to Orlando because I have a timeshare there. I stayed there for two days, visited Disney World, and then I left from Orlando and went to Cartagena. It saved me almost $800.

Try to be flexible with departing on different days of the week or times of the day. The price can be significantly lower. For instance, prices are usually higher to depart on a Friday, Monday and Sunday for domestic travel and any part of the weekend for international travel. Early morning or overnight flights are usually less. I have certainly aligned companies that I prefer when I travel, especially for international travel. I base this on the newness of the aircraft, seat comforts, entertainment, food and luggage allowance. **Seatguru.com** is a website I use to check any aircraft's information. You type in the airline and the aircraft model number. It will give you the seat layout, entertainment, year the aircraft was built, menu and if there are USB ports.

I fly Emirates and Qatar airlines as often as I can because of their customer service and the comfort of their aircrafts. They, along with Turkish Airlines, Ethiopian Airlines, Singapore Airlines, Etihad and Iceland Air, have great layover and stopover programs. These programs allow you to spend hours and days in the country or city with no additional airfare cost. I flew Turkish Airlines to Egypt and on my return flight home, the connecting flight to the USA was in Istanbul, Turkey. I was able to stay in Istanbul for two days and explore with no additional airline fees. In addition, I was also able to take advantage of the free city tour that's offered for anyone with a layover of more than six hours. Always check the airline's website for prices as well, then compare the price to sites like Expedia. Airlines do run sales quite often and they don't always announce them.

Join airline frequent flyer programs or apply for an airline credit card. As you earn miles, you qualify for upgrades and free travel.

You can transfer mileage and earn from one airline to another if they're affiliated. This way, you don't lose points. Transfer the points to the airline you use more frequently. I recently lost a thousand points on the airline Tap Portugal because I forgot to transfer my points to an affiliate airline I use more frequently.

It's very important to give yourself enough time between connecting flights. For domestic travel, schedule flights that have at least one hour before your connecting flight boards for departure. For international flights, allow no less than two hours. International airports are very large and confusing, and you may have difficulty finding your way around. Sometimes, the directions aren't clear, or they're not written in English. Your connecting flight may be on the other side of the airport. There are times when you must go through another or several security checkpoints. There are times when you may have to take a train or a bus to get to the next building where your flight is leaving from. When I was in Turkey, I had to go through four checkpoints before I got to my boarding gate, I had to literally run from one side of the airport to another in order to not miss my flight.

## ACCOMMODATIONS

When you're choosing your accommodations, research whether the hotel has the amenities you require. Look for the rating, is it five stars or three stars? Do you want luxury, moderate, or budget accommodations? Look at the pictures. Does it look well-kept? Are the furnishings modern? If you're considering a particular hotel, check several websites. Read the reviews of the previous guests thoroughly. You want to read the most recent and a few of the older ones. Look for bad reviews as well. This will give you a clue about issues and the facility's response. Check the map that the website provides of the facility's location. Is it close to attractions, the city center, the airport or is it far and isolated?

I suggest that you stay in brands that you know and are familiar with and not so isolated, at least until you become familiar with traveling alone. Solo travelers should be very cautious when choosing accommodations. Also, you want to research how you are going to get to your accommodations from the airport. Do you have to take a taxi? Do they have a pickup service? Do you have to take a flight? When I went to Belize, I had to take a small plane to get to my hotel destination. When I went to Venice, Italy, I had to take a boat from the airport, so if you're scared of small planes or if you don't like ferries because you get seasick easily, you need to take these things into consideration.

Purchasing bundle packages through sites like Expedia, TripAdvisor, booking.com, Priceline, group point, etc., may save you money and give you perks. As you accrue points from booking through these sites, you gain elite status, such a silver, gold, platinum, or VIP status. Your status determines the amount of the discounts you're eligible for. There are also perks, such as room upgrades on arrival, breakfast being included or other great discounts and giveaways.

Take note, if you're a rewards member of a brand hotel, Marriott or Hilton, and you book through one of these websites and not directly with the brand, you may forfeit your reward points for their program. If the price is cheaper on the website, contact the reservation line of the hotel directly and give them the price quoted by the other site and they will usually match it. This might be a time when you get a better deal booking hotel and airfare separately. There are certain brands that have bundle packages that include airfare and hotel. The Marriott and Hilton are two that I know of.

If you're not a rewards member of any hotel brand, I suggest you join at least one. I'm a member of a few. There are a lot of advantages to being a member, such as early check-in and late checkout, free room upgrades, breakfast, cocktail hour, and free transportation to and from the airport. You can also receive a free night for your birthday and anniversary gifts. For my birthday every year, the Marriot gifts me a free night hotel stay if I keep my reward counts at a certain status level.

## ALTERNATIVE ACCOMMODATIONS

Today, there are many options to choose from for people who have different preferences. Some like hotels. There are others that prefer a more private and intimate setting. Some like the feeling of being at home. Today, you can choose to sleep in luxury, moderate, and very untraditional accommodations. I'm only going to touch base on the most common ones.

### AIRBNB

This option allows you to have that home feeling. With Airbnb, you have the option of renting the entire space or a room sharing common areas. The location can be anywhere and as fancy or as common as you like it, ranging from various prices. The property can be a single dwelling, condominium, apartment or villa. Usually, they're operated by the owner and are very well maintained. You can pay them by the night instead of per person, lowering your cost and avoiding the single supplemental fee.

## On My Own

Always do your research on the location and what's included. In some places, you share a bathroom and there are no amenities. In other places, they don't service your room until you check out. If you need additional towels or service, there's a fee. They may or may not include breakfast. You also want to know if someone is available to assist you 24 hours a day with questions or concerns and do they assist or provide transportation to their location from the airport, bus or train station, etc.

I'm a luxury traveler and prefer luxury hotel accommodations. When I went to Marrakesh, Morocco, I wanted to experience staying in a riad, which is a traditional Moroccan home. I spent part of my time in a luxury hotel and then I rented a room with a private bath in a riad. I researched thoroughly and chose a riad through Airbnb based on reviews.

The host was listed as a super host, which means the property consistently got excellent reviews. This place was absolutely beautiful. Very clean and well-furnished; the architecture was mind-blowing. The owner was so kind and very helpful. He arranged my transportation, assisted me with excursions and cooked breakfast each morning. The only problem was the location. It was outside of the Medina walls, in a residential neighborhood, but the area was a little rough looking, especially for a woman traveling solo.

He realized how nervous I was and took excellent care of me. He would call a taxi for me and walk me to it. He would text me while I was out to make sure I was okay. He would have a car come and transport me back from the Medina and he waited outside for me no matter how late it was. I felt very safe inside my accommodations and there were other guests to mingle with. Some of them felt the same about the area as well. I will return to this riad because of the excellent customer service of the host and now I know what to expect.

My experience in Cuba was completely different. I rented an apartment through Airbnb. I did my research thoroughly and read the reviews, the apartment was located on the top floor of a mansion in a residential neighborhood in Havana, it was breathtaking with immaculate marble floors and walls. The neighborhood was very safe. I walked outside very late at night alone and was never bothered unless someone was just trying to see if I needed assistance. The owner of this home was also very kind and resourceful. Two totally different experiences with locations.

## BED AND BREAKFAST

Bed and breakfasts are usually large homes that rent out bedrooms or a guest house. Some are very unique places to stay. You might have a room with a private bath or must share one with other guests. The owners usually reside in the home or on the property. Meals are usually included. They're usually located farther away from the city.

## HOSTELS

A hostel is a low-budget accommodation that's a shared space. Basically, you're renting a bed in a room with as little as 4 people or as many as 20. It's structured like a college dorm, including the bathroom setup. If lack of privacy isn't an issue for you, this might interest you. Take note that most don't supply towels or toiletries. Hostels are very popular in Europe and are usually located in major cities. Some serve breakfast or have a fully equipped kitchen that allows you to cook your own meals. A lot of them are in areas close to many attractions, restaurants and nightlife. Be careful some of these hostels are located in very old buildings and not-so-great areas. Do your research just like you would for any accommodation. I have never stayed in one but have met many ladies while traveling that have, they had both positive and negative experiences. I guess there are pros and cons to anything.

## BOUTIQUE HOTELS

This is my favorite type of accommodation. When I went to Venice and Rome, most of the brand hotels were far from the city center. I wanted to be directly in the city. A friend recommended these boutique hotels she stayed in. I researched both hotels and booked them. They were both amazing and in excellent, very safe locations. However, they were quite different in appearance. The one in Venice was very charming. It was in a very old building with luxurious antique furnishing. The one in Rome was also in a very old building but had been gutted and was very modern inside with an art deco style. I love the attention boutique hotels provide. They're small and usually go above and beyond to make your stay wonderful. I was also surprised at the amenities that they offered. Boutique hotels vary in price range, the two I stayed in were luxury rated. There are boutique hotels that have budget and moderate price ranges as well. Remember to always do your research. There are many websites to assist you with information about accommodations.

## ALL-INCLUSIVE RESORTS

All-inclusive are like hotels but usually have so many amenities that you may never want to leave the resort during your stay. They can be budget, moderate or luxury. The great thing is everything is included. You pay one price, and you don't have to worry about food, drinks or entertainment. Usually, there are lots of activities included. Some resorts include gratuity, so you don't have to be concerned about tipping. You're free to go and just enjoy your stay. Not much planning is involved. I think all-inclusive resorts are great for solo travelers just starting out or for someone that just wants to relax and not do a whole lot.

I know some of you are thinking about the large families and children that usually frequent all-inclusive resorts. There are several resorts that are for adults only and don't just cater to couples. I stayed solo at Sandals Resort in St. Lucia and had a wonderful time. There were other solo travelers there. I met some very exciting people from different countries that I'm still in contact with. The resort was so luxurious and had everything I needed. I only went into town once to buy souvenirs. The package I bought through Sandals included my airfare as well.

One of the cons of all-inclusive resorts is that they can limit your ability to experience the true culture of the country you're visiting. You may be so comfortable at the resort that you're reluctant to go off the property to explore. If you're going on vacation just to relax and have "me time", this might be just the thing you need.

Research is key when choosing your accommodations. There are pros and cons to any type. The most important thing is your safety. Please don't put your safety at risk to save money on accommodations or stay somewhere too isolated off the grid for peace and quiet.

## TRAVEL INSURANCE

I cannot express the importance of travel insurance enough. Please don't exclude it. If you must take something off the list, choose another item. Your loss could be much greater than the money you think you will save. Imagine being in a foreign country with a medical emergency. The cost can be astronomical, especially if you're in an intensive care unit. Trying to get out of a country with other disasters, such as a hurricane, is chaotic enough, but canceled flights or having to evacuate your beachfront hotel is even worse. Travel insurance covers these items. Travel insurance can reimburse you for travel plans that must be canceled due to illness or family emergencies. You can also get medical evacuation insurance. This insurance will ensure you can be flown home with a medical team if you are too sick to travel on your own. Worst case scenario, it will also help cover expenses to bring your body home in case of death. I know we don't want to think about death going on vacation, but these things unexpectedly happen. I've heard so many heart breaking stories of families having to pay thousands of dollars to bring to their loved ones home.

There are many travel insurance agencies to choose from. You should purchase your insurance as soon as you book your travel. Travel insurance included in credit card purchases is usually basic and doesn't cover all your needs. Always explain your travel itinerary thoroughly to the agent. If you scuba dive, make sure you get a policy that covers that. If you skydive or hike mountains, make sure your policy covers that. Understand the limits of the policy before you purchase it. Read thoroughly through the policies on pregnancy, age limitation, and pre-existing medical conditions. Traveling is wonderful, but we sometimes don't prepare for unexpected events. Don't let your wonderful memories be ruined by not having the coverage for the unexpected, this should also include Covid travel insurance. This insurance is separate from regular travel insurance. You want to make sure that you're covered with Covid for cancellation of your trip, but also for medical coverage if you develop Covid while you're on vacation.

## SINGLE SUPPLEMENT

A single supplement is a charge for solo travelers staying in a room alone. Most accommodations are based on double occupancy. This is standard for hotels, some cruise lines and some excursions as well. As stated earlier in the budget section, plan to include this fee. I'm finding the more I travel, the more the single supplement fee has been decreasing and some vendors have removed it altogether. This is a great thing because statistics show 45% of people that travel for leisure are solo travelers. A way to beat this is to join hotel reward programs. You can get them to reduce or move the single supplement or upgrade you to upset the cost. I find a lot of niceness without acting entitled goes a long way. I usually get whatever I ask for through loyalty programs.

## HIGH VERSUS LOW SEASON

The least expensive time to travel to any destination is in their low season. Prices are less and so are the crowds. When there are no crowds, the hotels are willing to give free upgrades and other enticements to get your business. Also, the staff can be more attentive when guest registration is slow.

You can always expect to pay more for traveling during spring break, the winter holidays and certain parts of the summer. Prices for the Caribbean decrease as hurricane season approaches. The same for tropical countries that experience monsoon and rainy seasons.

Each country has a different high, mid, and low season. Research your destination to find out about their different seasons. When

## On My Own

I went to Egypt, I went during the low season, which is June to August. It's extremely hot, especially in upper Egypt. Even though that was a luxury trip for me, it was still very affordable because of the time of year I went. If I had gone during peak season, which is mid-October to May with cooler weather, the price would've been doubled. There's a good and a bad side to this. I saved a lot of money, but the weather was dangerously hot. My tour guide scheduled all my tours for early in the morning and I had to make sure I stayed hydrated. I was at a tour site between 7:00 AM and 8:00 AM. I was usually back at my hotel or cruise ship before 2:00 PM. This gave me the rest of the day to enjoy the amenities of the hotel or cruise ship and take a nap to get ready for the nightlife. Because there were no crowds, I was also able to take my time, walk around, and admire all the artifacts. My pictures were also amazing! No unwanted people. Thank you!

CHAPTER 7

# Solo Cruising

*"You never really travel alone. The world is full of friends waiting to get to know you."*

Cruising solo can be one of the best things for solo travelers, especially a beginner. There are many options for the length of cruises. You can choose three-, four-, five- and seven-day cruises. Most cruise ships today are enormous. They're like floating cities with numerous attractions and activities on board. You can participate in everything or nothing at all. You never have to leave the ship if you don't want to.

What I love about cruises is you can visit several destinations in one trip. You're only there for a short period of time. This is not good if you really like the destination. However, if you don't like the destination, at least you're not stuck there for a week. I have flown to an island before and did not like it at all. I had to tough it out for five long days. After that incident, I started cruising again for many years. The destinations I loved, I put them on my bucket list to return and stay a few days.

There are many cruise lines to choose from to fit any budget. You don't have to pay all at once. You can make a deposit and they will let you know when it must be paid in full. Many cruise lines are making solo cruising more affordable. 20 to 25% of passengers on all cruise ships are solo travelers, and these numbers are on the rise. Since the world has opened back up to travel after the long Covid pandemic, solo travel is the way of the future. People are eager to travel again. Then, there are those who only dreamed about traveling, realizing time waits for no one. They now see the world can shut down again for any reason at any time. They're quickly making reservations to travel. People are not waiting or trying to convince family and friends to travel with them.

Many cruise lines have reduced the single supplement charge. Usually, you must pay for the entire cabin, which is double occupancy, when traveling solo. Some cruise lines have added studio cabins to certain ships in their fleets to accommodate solo travelers. The rooms are smaller than the regular cabins but still have everything you need. These rooms fill up quickly because of high demand. They usually never go on sale.

Don't know where to start? To pick a cruise line, begin with online reviews. Ask for reviews from family and friends that have cruised before. Know your reason for wanting to travel. Currently, different cruise lines have different vibes and themes. What's your budget? I've been on several cruise lines with family and friends, but here I will mention the cruise lines I've been on solo and my experience.

**CARNIVAL CRUISE LINE** is known as the fun ship. If you're a social butterfly or at least ready to be one, I highly recommend cruising at least once with this cruise line. They have many ships to choose from with different themes. I find their rooms a little smaller than some of the other cruise lines. They're still well-decorated and have what you need. There's always a party and lots of fun on board. Nonstop fast-paced and active fun. I love playing bingo and being involved in scavenger hunt games or trivia. The deck parties are a blast. I have never had a dull moment and I have been on many Carnival cruises. I've cried once while de-boarding. I had so much fun and met the most amazing people, and the staff was phenomenal. I wasn't ready to go home.

**ROYAL CARIBBEAN CRUISE LINE** is the driving innovation of the sea. Their ships are massive and architectural marvels, with great cuisine. There are many specialty restaurants on board. Delicious is an understatement. However, they're not all included in the price of the cruise. There's a main dining room that serves breakfast, lunch and dinner that's included in your price. Please check the website thoroughly or call and ask which restaurants are included.

They do offer pre-cruise packages for these specialty restaurants, beverages, Wi-Fi, photography, shore excursions, spa, etc... I highly suggest you prepay for everything on any cruise line. The prices are higher once you board the ship, and your desired time slot may not be available. It's great to prepay so you can enjoy your time doing activities instead of standing in line or being surprised at your bill the night before departing the ship. I've seen many people not be able to depart the ship because they have an outstanding balance they can't afford to cover.

Royal Caribbean has two private islands that are very beautiful. Coco Cay in The Bahamas and the other is in Labadee, Haiti. They're exclusive to Royal Caribbean cruise ships. So overcrowding is not an issue. There's food, shopping and lots of water activities, or you can simply enjoy the beach. The entertainment on this cruise line is great too. There's so much to do on these ships, such as ice skating, rock climbing, carousels, zipline, wave pools, laser tag, flow riders, parades, miniature golf, mystery dinners, a card room and so much more. You can cruise for seven days and not be able to venture the entire ship. I have stayed on the ship at ports of call that I have been to previously just to enjoy the amenities of the ship. It's less crowded.

**DISNEY CRUISE LINE** is amazing, period. Some people find it expensive, but as far as I'm concerned, nobody does it like Disney. The customer service is phenomenal. Disney is also known for its ships, great decor, themes and large cabins. It has the most enchanted entertainment. The cuisine is great with the best desserts. I know you think about kids being everywhere. Not true. Disney cruise line has adult-only areas. Disney also has a private island in the Bahamas called Castaway Cay. It's so beautiful, and it's broken into areas, family area, adults only, and teenagers only. Yes, teenagers have their own special area. I have been on many Disney cruises, but only solo once. I really enjoyed myself. I'm a Disney fanatic. I love Mickey Mouse and he can do no wrong in my eyes.

**VIRGIN VOYAGE CRUISE LINE** is an adult-only cruise line. You must be 18 years and older to get on board. It has a super yacht-inspired atmosphere and focuses on health and wellness. I love that it's all-inclusive, including Wi-Fi and non-alcoholic beverages. There are no surprises.

A travel agent can provide great information and they can assist you with booking. You can also book directly with the cruise lines. Check the cruise line's website to inquire about solo traveler supplements or cabins offered. You can also call them, speaking to a customer service agent may be better for your questions. Look at the ports of call they offer and when they're available. You can also get an idea of what each ship offers and the layout. Most cruise lines will assist you with booking your air travel.

For cheap fares, you may get a reduced rate on last-minute cruise deals for standard rooms. Sometimes, cruise lines will reduce the price or waive the supplement fee to fill the ship. Try cruising off-peak season. Make sure you buy insurance just in case of inclement weather.

Once you pick a cruise line, join their rewards program. You get reward points for each sale and some nice perks. Things like early boarding and departure, discounts, excursions, specialty restaurants, cabin upgrades, and much more.

## WHAT TO DO TO PREVENT LONELINESS

Get to know the crew. They will keep you informed on the happenings on the ship. They're also from all around the globe and love talking to you about their homeland and the families they leave behind.

Hang out in the public spaces on the ship. It's a great way to meet new people.

## On My Own

Check the program that's placed in your stateroom each evening. It has the next day's itinerary and activities listed. I'm sure you'll find something that strikes your attention.

Sign up for assigned seating time. You will be placed at a table with other people rather than dining alone. You will eat with the same group of people for the duration of the cruise and the same waiters. You can always change this arrangement if it doesn't work for you.

Participate in shore excursions. They're safe and put together by the cruise line. If something happens and the excursion is late returning you to the ship, the ship must wait, or they're responsible for getting you to the next port of call. I have made many lasting friends on shore excursions. Everyone is excited to explore.

Remember, researching and educating yourself is the key to a positive and wonderful adventure.

# Solo Cruising

CHAPTER 8

# Safety Is Always First

*"May your journey be free from stress and bring you home safely."*

Safety should be the number one priority, whether you're traveling alone or with a group. People ask me all the time if I'm scared to travel solo, and my answer is no. Terrible things can happen to you anywhere and regardless of whether you're alone or in a group. Just look at all the terrible incidents that have happened in the United States over the past years. There have been bombings, school shootings, church shootings and massive shootings at concerts. Are you accompanied every time you leave your home or when you're at home? The same safety measures you take on an everyday basis are the same safety measures you take while traveling with a little more emphasis. Let's discuss them.

- Once you have decided on your destination, check with the US Embassy on the travel conditions of the country you plan to visit.
- Is the country safe?
- Are there any political challenges there right now?
- What is their relationship with your country?
- Research the customs, culture, dress code religion and basic laws and become familiar with them.
- You don't want to be arrested or fined in a foreign country, especially for something you may think is very trivial. What you may think is very simple can be a big deal somewhere else.

I almost got a fine for chewing gum in Singapore while I was there on a layover. I didn't know it was illegal to chew gum there. Luckily the police officer was very nice and made sure I disposed of it properly. This could have cost me a lot of money, including the cost of missing my flight.

- Register with the Smart Traveler Enrollment Program (STEP), https://step.state.gov. Once registered, the embassy will notify you if safety conditions have changed prior to your travel or during your visit. They will help you get to a safe place until they can assist you to get out of that country. This also includes catastrophic conditions as well. They will also help your family contact you if there's an emergency at home.

- Make two colored copies of the demographic page of your passport. Take one with you and keep it separate from your original passport. You should also take a picture of it with your phone. Never walk around with your passport book while sightseeing. Leave it in the safe at your hotel. Carry the copy with you. Leave the other copy at home with a family member or friend along with a copy of your complete itinerary.

- Wear a medical bracelet if you have a medical condition or keep a note in your wallet about your condition along with allergies you may have. List the medications you're currently taking. If the country's primary language isn't English, it would be very beneficial to have the note written in their language. **Google Translate** can help you with that. Pack a small first aid kit and take prophylactic medications for an upset stomach, food poisoning, etc.

- Keep in touch with family and friends. I always get an international plan with my cell phone service provider. This allows me to call home every day, text and send photos without roaming fees. Some people change out their phone sim card but there's too much scamming going on. I don't want to risk my phone being stolen or compromised. I call my daughter daily to remind her of my plans or if I've changed them at all. I'll also send a few photos throughout the day via text and inform her when I've returned to my room for the night. This is a safety measure. It gives her a trail to follow in case something happens. Check with your cell phone provider about international plans that they may offer. You can also use **WhatsApp** to talk to your family and friends.

- Have the hotel make arrangements to pick you up from the airport, bus or train station. If you decide to use an outside source, make sure the referral is from people you know and trust and have used that service. An added safety precaution I use is not to let them put my actual name on the card or banner they hold up. I give them a nickname, or something made up. This way I know it's definitely the transportation arranged for me.

You can also have the driver call the hotel desk before you enter the vehicle and speak with someone there as a precaution. Most countries have **Google Maps** now. Download it prior to your travel date, plug in the hotel address if it's available, and you can see if the taxi is going in the right direction or even taking the best route. I used this in Spain, Morocco, and Italy recently. You will find most transport drivers using an internet map system as well. It offers travel directions for driving, walking and public transportation. It's a wonderful app to keep you from getting lost and pulling out paper maps, marking you as a tourist.

- Program local emergency numbers into your phone, including your hotel. If they have a business card at the desk with the address and phone number, take one and place it in your pocket or somewhere separate from your wallet. If your wallet gets lost or stolen or your phone battery dies, you can still contact the hotel for assistance if needed.

- Avoid ground floor rooms. They're most susceptible to break-ins. The safest floors are from the fourth to the sixth floor. High enough for people not to climb up through the window and low enough for you to exit quickly in case of a fire or other safety issues. Also, avoid rooms next to the elevator. Mid hallway is the best. You will have more time to know if you're being followed and have time to react.

- Never tell anyone you meet where you're staying. Lie and tell them a different location. Never tell people you're alone. Ladies, wear a ring that looks like a wedding band. Tell people that your husband is in the room, or your family didn't want to join you for this activity. Tell them you'll be meeting up with them later. Once you're sure that a person is okay, then you can give them some information but not all.

## On My Own

- Keep your door always locked and double-bolted. Put the security chain on. I have invested in a travel door wedge with an alarm. It makes a very loud noise if someone attempts to enter. There are several types. I brought mine off **Amazon**. Also, cover the peephole. Sometimes they're not a one-way device.

- Never give your credit card or personal information over the phone in the hotel if someone says they're calling from the front desk and that there's a problem with your credit card or information. Tell them you will come to the desk to handle it. Thieves call random hotel rooms to steal information. Chances are you will go to the desk, and they won't know what you're talking about.

- Please mind the culture of the country you're visiting and dress appropriately. For women solo travelers, you want to blend in. Don't wear expensive-looking jewelry. You don't want to stand out and draw unwanted attention to yourself. Be mindful of displays of affection in public if you meet someone. In some countries, inappropriate dress and public displays of affection will land you in jail. Always pack a couple of long dresses or pants with shirts or blouses with at least mid-sleeve. Ladies, pack a shawl or a sarong if you plan on visiting temples or other sacred landmarks to cover your hair and other exposed areas. Make sure your dresses are not too sheer. You will not be allowed into these sacred places if you're not dressed appropriately. Some temples and mosques have these items for rent, but not all. So come prepared.

- Be aware of the pickpockets. They're everywhere. There are usually warning signs posted in areas that have a high incidence of pickpockets. Try to blend in and not look so touristy. Leave your expensive items at home. Don't wear expensive-looking jewelry. Even your cell phone is not safe. Buy a phone case that a lanyard can be attached. This allows you to wear it around your neck and place it under your shirt or blouse, out of sight when not in use. These people are very creative and will cause a scene to get you off guard to rob you. They use children as well to get your attention. Children will come up to you and pretend to be lost or hurt. Don't assist them. It may be a setup for a pickpocket or robbery attempt. Walk away, go into a store and ask them to help. Or if you see law enforcement, get their attention to get them involved.

- Invest in a money belt that can be hidden under your clothing. Wear clothing that may have many pockets and zippers. If you carry a backpack, make sure it has many hidden compartments on the inside and the straps are cut-proof. I carry an across-the-shoulder bag that has many compartments. The strap has metal wiring inside and is cut-proof. I purchased it from **Amazon**. Cutting the straps to a backpack or purse is a regular routine of thieves in crowded places.

- Don't carry a lot of cash. Separate your money keeping the smaller bills in one area and the larger bills in another area on your person. If you use an ATM, make sure it's in a safe and secure location. Become familiar with the local currency and the exchange rate. I use an app called **Currency Converter Pro** by Apple. When you make a purchase, be sure to secure your wallet and or change as discreetly as you can. Don't rush or allow yourself to become distracted. Make sure strangers are not too close in your personal space.

- Learn key words and phrases of the primary language. This is very important for safety and just to show respect for the culture. Simple phrases such as, thank you, please, I need help, where's the bathroom, I'm lost, I feel sick. You can also use translator apps like **Google Translate**. The app allows you to download the language of the country you plan to visit prior to leaving. If you download it, you'll be able to translate information without the internet. **YouTube** has many channels that give lessons for travel in various languages. I have learned basic French, Arabic, Italian, and Portuguese from watching YouTube. I'm also fluent in Spanish.

- Trust your instincts. If something doesn't feel right, it probably isn't. Have your room changed or change hotels. You must feel comfortable and safe where you're staying.

**Safety Is Always First**

CHAPTER 9

# It's All About The Money

*"Travel because money can always return. Time will not."*

Exchanging money in foreign countries makes a lot of people nervous. I must admit, I was very afraid in the beginning and made some expensive mistakes. This is why I added this chapter. I don't want you to make the same mistakes. Exchanging money is not difficult. Education and research are the master keys, as with everything in life.

When you're choosing your destination, look and compare the value of your country's currency to the country you're planning to visit. This is called the exchange rate. If your country's currency is less than the country you plan to visit, you will lose some money. Depending on how low the exchange rate is, you may want to change the destination and visit the other location when the exchange rates are better.

I went to London in 2019. The exchange rate of the USD compared to the British Pound was horrible. I lost money on the exchange. I couldn't cancel because this was a business trip. 1 British Pound (GBP) at the time was equal to $1.31 USD. If I exchanged $500 USD, I would only receive 350 British pounds. A loss of $150 USD. Then there are the fees associated with the exchange. They're different depending on where you do the transaction. That just gives you an idea of the loss. I planned and increased my budget for this trip. I kept track of my expenditures that could be written off as business expenses. At the time I didn't know I could have used my debit card at an ATM for cash and saved money. Sometimes, you learn as you go. The great thing is my bank doesn't charge fees for international ATM use. I'll talk more about this later in the chapter.

When I went to Bali, Indonesia, I was very happy with the exchange rate. 1 USD was equivalent to 15,190.32 Indonesian Rupiah (IDR). I lived very well on that nine-day holiday. I did lots of shopping and still came home with more than half of my spending budget.

People ask me all the time if they should exchange money prior to their trip. I say yes, you should always have some currency from the country you're visiting on you prior to your arrival. This will give you time to become familiar with the currency, like the different denominations. You will have money on hand to get something to eat, pay for a taxi or transportation and even tip if needed. The worst thing you can do is exchange currency at the airport terminals. It's very convenient, but it's not worth the price. Airport kiosks offer rates that are much worse than the true exchange rate. You can lose as much as 25% of your money when you exchange currency at the airport. This should be your last resort and only exchange enough until you can get to a currency exchange booth with better exchange rates. I always ask the local workers at my hotel where the best place to exchange money is. Many of them receive funding from family members in the United States and other countries. They're usually very familiar with which places have the best exchange rates. There are also other options.

Call your bank or credit union branch to order the currency. A bank or credit union will offer its customers the best exchange rate. However, there's usually a flat rate fee for them doing the leg work for you. They will tell you which branch location you can pick it from if they don't have it. They can also ship it directly to your home if you live in the United States. Most institutions may require up to at least 10 business days. So, order it as soon as possible. I have done this many times. I like to have some cash on hand and only use my credit cards when necessary. You can exchange the currency you don't use before you leave the country or when you return. I always keep some as souvenirs.

If you carry cash abroad, make sure the bills are new and crisp. Foreign banks and businesses will not accept worn or wrinkled bills. When you receive change, check the bills to ensure they're not worn or torn. You will not be able to exchange them.

Using ATMs is another option. Inquire if your bank or credit union charges foreign transaction fees to use your card at international ATMs. If they don't, then it will be cheaper to get cash from the ATM versus exchanging your cash. Research and find the best credit or debit card option for you. A friend I met in Portugal told me about Charles Swab Banking. After researching the information, I opened a checking account with them. They don't charge foreign transaction fees. They also reimburse all my ATM fees. Airline credit cards usually don't charge foreign transaction fees either. Plus, they have lots of other perks. Just remember to use safety measures when using ATMs. Watch your surroundings and your personal space and make sure you're in a safe location. Never put all your money in one area.

Remember to notify your financial institution and credit card company of your travel plans. If not, you risk the chance of having your credit card locked due to suspicious activity. Ask them for their international customer service number. Take a picture of the front and back of your card or store it in the wallet app of your cell phone. Don't forget to ask what the daily withdrawal limits are. Change your daily limits as well on your debit card. I usually decrease my daily limit on my debit card and take a high-limit credit card and one with a smaller limit. I have one card that's specifically used for travel. I pay it off after each trip. I start each trip with a zero balance, and I always have some cash on hand.

When I was in Bali, a waitress accidentally ran my card for one million US dollars instead of Indonesian Rupiah. That's roughly sixty-five US dollars. I ate a lot of food and plus I treated my tour guide to dinner. Still a very inexpensive meal with lobster and shrimp. She was new. It was an honest mistake. However, my card was locked due to fraudulent activity. I called the bank immediately to explain the situation and answered every security question. They would not unlock that card. They cancelled it and sent a new one to my home in the United States. Thank goodness I had another card to use and cash. It was only my second day there with seven more to go. The waitress felt so bad and was embarrassed. The owner wanted to waive the cost of the meal, but I paid anyway. Always have cash on hand and at least two credit cards in case of incidents.

Research if the country you're traveling to is credit card friendly or if your bank will allow you to use your debit card in that country prior to making travel arrangements. Fraud is on the rise; some banks will not allow you to use a debit card in certain countries. The USA also has sanctions on certain countries Cuba, for example. You cannot use a credit card from a USA bank in Cuba. You must use cash.

Mastercard and Visa are widely accepted abroad. American Express isn't as popular in some countries. I still never leave home without it. There are a lot of perks that come with that card. Discover Card is basically unheard of outside of the United States. Small businesses and street merchants may not accept any credit cards. So, always have some cash on hand.

*"You must do the research. If you don't know about something, then ask the right people who do."*
**Spike Lee**

**It's All About The Money**

CHAPTER 10

# The Packing Saga And Luggage Wars

*"He would travel happily must travel light."*
**Antione de St Exupery**

The thought of going on vacation is fun and exciting. However, when it's time to pack, the struggle begins. Even seasoned travelers struggle with packing, but there are many travelers that have mastered the art of carry-on luggage. I have a friend that can do a 14-day trip and never check luggage. I'm not that girl. I can do a three-to-four-day trip with carry-on luggage. If the trip is longer, I need to check at least one bag. I'm that girl that used to take a suitcase for shoes, another suitcase for my regular clothing and a garment bag for my evening attire for a seven-day cruise. I know it's a bit much, but I bet a few of you can relate.

I hate getting to a destination and needing to buy clothing or essential items that I left behind. It's also a challenge if you have allergies and must use certain brands or special personal items. You don't know if you'll be able to purchase them at your destination. Besides, there are just certain things a girl can't go without. Packing can be aggravating for many, but you will be happier if you take your time and do it right. It will save you money and frustration.

I was forced to learn that the less you take the better. Many European countries require you to climb a lot of stairs. Most accommodations don't have elevators. If they do, they may not always be in working order. If you have many pieces of luggage, or if your luggage is heavy, you must be able to manage it. There may not be anyone to help you, especially if you arrive late in the evening. Remember, you're alone.

I went on a five-country trip for over a month. I had two large suitcases plus my personal bag. I arrived late in the afternoon in Portugal. I was staying in a beautiful boutique hotel. The elevator was broken. My room was three flights up. Thank goodness another guest offered to help. I treated him to breakfast the next morning.

In Venice, Italy, I stayed at another beautiful boutique hotel. There was no elevator. I arrived late at night. They left the room key for me with a note at the desk. I had to carry those bags up two flights of stairs. I carried one up and went back down for the other. I was so exhausted and out of breath afterwards. All I could do was drink water and lay down for a few minutes to get my composure.

In Greece, there are many hills. You may have to go downstairs to check in to your hotel, then walk back upstairs, and back down again to get to your room. Trust me, I learned to pack much lighter and investigate the hotel's layout more thoroughly.

## CHOOSE YOUR LUGGAGE

First, you must decide on the type of luggage to take with you. This will depend on your destination and length of stay. If you're traveling to a warm climate, your clothes will be lighter and require a smaller suitcase. If the climate is cold, then you will need to carry a larger suitcase.

Today, there are so many options with luggage. There's the traditional suitcase, garment bags that fold and have wheels, and I see more people with backpacks. When choosing your luggage, consider durability, size, weight and its wheels. It's much easier to maneuver a suitcase that has spinning wheels than one that just rolls. If it expands and has compartments, that's awesome. I also suggest you buy a different color than black. Tie a bright color handkerchief around the handle or some other object. It helps to Identify your luggage quickly. It's such a bummer when you think it's your suitcase on the carousel and you quickly discover it's not.

## MAKE A LIST

Make a list and pack according to your itinerary. If you're lying on a beach all day, then you will need more swimwear than clothing. Don't forget about the dress codes of places you may want to visit. Temples, restaurants, churches or other historical sites may require you to dress modestly. I always pack a shawl to cover my arms and a dress or skirt that goes below my knees. Pack clothes that you can mix and match.

Don't over pack. I promise you won't wear half of the clothing anyway. My golden rule is to start packing days before your trip and not the night before. Go through the items again in a day or two. There's a 90% chance you will remove items that you realize you can do without. Every item in your suitcase should serve a purpose.

## BUNDLE YOUR OUTFITS

I like to be organized. I find bundling my outfits helps to prevent wrinkles and easily identifies items I've packed. Simply roll your pant and shirt with your undergarments into one bundle. It keeps your suitcase neat and allows you to grab a bundle knowing you have a complete outfit.

## BUY WRINKLE-PROOF FABRICS

I love linen clothing. However, it's a disaster for travel. It wrinkles as soon as you sit down and takes a long-time ironing or steaming to get the wrinkles out. Try purchasing polyester, spandex, denim, lyocell, rayon and permanent-press items. You can fold and roll these items without difficulty to give more space in your luggage.

## PACK COMFORTABLE SHOES

Ladies, some of us love our heels. Depending on your destination, they may not be safe to wear. Many European countries have cobblestone streets. In some countries, the streets are poorly paved. It's very easy to fall or twist your ankle. If you want to wear heels, wedge heels are better than stilettos. Shoes are also bulky and heavy; they take up a lot of space and add excess weight to your luggage.

## TRAVEL COMPRESSION BAGS AND PACKING CUBES

I love travel compression bags. They protect your clothing and will compress items to help you save space in your luggage. They're sealable plastic bags with one-way pressure valves that let air out but not in. When you remove the air, your clothes are compressed. They come in different sizes. Some also come with a pump to remove the air. There are others where you just roll the bag to release the air. I usually use them when I want to do carry-on luggage. These are also great when you travel in the cooler months with bulkier clothing. Placing these bulky items in a compression bag will save space in your suitcase. I have purchased them from **Amazon** and **TJ Max**.

Packing cubes help you to pack more efficiently. Organize the cubes by types of clothing and essential items. Place items in cubes according to your itinerary. Packing cubes help your suitcase remain neat and organized. You don't have to dig around or take many items to find what you need. I like to use them for my shoes, toiletries and swimwear. They come in different colors and sets with different sizes. I also buy these from **Amazon**, but many other stores and online shops carry them. A very inexpensive way to protect your clothing from your shoes is to wrap them in shower caps.

## THE PILLOWCASE HACK

I learned this neat idea from a woman on Tik Tok. You need one pillowcase with a zipper and another one without. Place clothing in the zippered pillowcase and then cover it with the other pillowcase. I've also taken the stuffing out of a decorative couch pillow that has a zipper and stuffed it with clothing. This is a great hack. You have a pillow to sleep with. You also have clothing with you in case your luggage is lost or delayed. Most airlines don't count your pillow as a carry-on.

## KEEP YOUR CLOTHES FRESH

I always carry a laundry bag with me. You can buy one that folds into a small pouch with a zipper. I use it to keep my clean and dirty clothes separated. Sometimes you're not able to do laundry before you travel home. Placing cinnamon sticks or lavender satchels in your luggage will help to keep it smelling fresh.

## TAKE PHOTOS OF YOUR LUGGAGE

Once you're packed, take photos of the inside of the suitcase prior to closing it. Take pictures of all sides of your luggage while closed. This will help you with insurance claims if your luggage is lost or damaged. Take photos of the serial numbers of your electronics as well. Many travelers are now using Air Tags or smart tags to track the items themselves if they become lost.

## WHAT TO PLACE IN YOUR PERSONAL BAG

Pack your passport, travel documents and medication in your personal bag. Never in checked luggage or a carry-on bag. Sometimes, the airline may need you to check your carry-on luggage for any number of reasons. In a haste, you forget to remove these items. Your passport should always be with you when traveling internationally. You also need it to get through Customs and Immigration.

Make sure to pack your medication and place it in your personal item bag. You should carry them in the prescribed bottle for international travel. Take more than you think you need, except for narcotics. Customs needs to be able to easily identify the medication. If you take too many narcotics, they may think you're going to sell them. They will confiscate them. Research your medications and make sure they're not illegal in the country you're visiting. The customs agents may take them and not return them or even deny your entrance.

The most forgotten items are cell phone chargers and cords for cameras, computers and video cameras. Charge everything up the night before and place the cords in your personal bag. Some hotels have extra from guests that have left them behind. Some will rent one to you. Just ask before you buy one.

Invest in a travel adaptor. Most countries use a different voltage than the United States. Hotels don't always have them for rent or purchase. The good thing is that USB ports are easily found. Charging your phone or iPad is not an issue, but your laptop or camera will be if you don't have a converter. You can purchase converters cheaply now from **Target, Amazon, Best Buy, Walmart**, etc.

Another great investment is a travel battery charger for your cell phone, headset, selfie stick or camera. If you're constantly using them while out on an excursion, the battery dies quickly. There may be no place to recharge. Most tour guides carry one, but there's nothing like having your own. Research them. They come in different sizes and milliamps. You can search online to find the type that works for you.

## LUGGAGE FEES

I spoke earlier about including checked luggage in your travel budget. The airline makes a fortune from luggage fees yearly, somewhere to the tune of billions of dollars.

Before you hit the purchase button to buy your airline ticket be sure to check the baggage fees. Based on the class of ticket you buy; you may be allotted one free checked bag. Sometimes two, depending on the airline and your destination. Always check the weight limit and the overweight fee. If your bag is overweight, you must remove the excess or pay an overweight fee. This fee can be a hundred dollars or more. You may find it more economically feasible to purchase the next class ticket rather than pay for checked luggage. Remember, the fee is for departure and your return.

Carry-on luggage must adhere to a certain weight and size. Most airlines are now weighing carry-on bags. If your luggage is overweight or too big, they will make you check it. If your carry-on bag doesn't fit in their prototype for carry-on items, you must pay a fee. Some of the low-cost airlines charge a carry-on fee if you purchase a basic economy ticket.

To avoid fees here are a few things you can do:

- Research airlines that don't charge a fee for at least the first checked bag. Sometimes, you may benefit by upgrading your ticket to the next class to avoid baggage fees. Do what is more affordable for you.
- If you travel frequently, fly with one airline and join its rewards program so that you can earn elite status. You can also fly with its affiliates and transfer points to gain elite status faster. There are many airlines that don't charge elite members for checked luggage.
- Apply for an airline visa or master credit card that has baggage benefits. Your purchases will give you points towards luggage, upgrades and free tickets.
- Carry on your luggage. Pack very light, use travel cubes and compression bags to make room in your suitcase. Always check with the airline about weight and size proportions. When I carry on my luggage, I use a regular-size backpack as my personal item. You would be surprised by the amount of stuff you can fit in it. The great thing is if you have it on your back, the ticket agent hardly ever sees it to ask you to weigh it.
- If all else fails, budget for checked luggage. Purchase a luggage scale and weigh your luggage prior to arriving at the airport. Remove any excess weight. Scales are very inexpensive and they're portable. I purchased mine at Bed, Bath and Beyond for $15 dollars.
- At the luggage counter, make sure to inquire that your luggage is checked through to your final destination. If not, you may have to pay additional fees. Research will save you time and money.

**The Packing Saga And Luggage Wars**

*"On a long journey even a straw weighs heavy."*
**Spanish Proverb**

# On My Own

CHAPTER 11

# Let's Go Take Pictures And Explore

*"Fill Your life with adventure not things, have stories to tell not stuff to show."*

## PHOTOGRAPHY

People always ask who takes my pictures. I use tripods, the help of strangers, my tour guide and I hire professional photographers. I wrote a blog that gives a lot of details about it at **pacnplay.com.**

I invested in two tripods. I purchased both on **Amazon**. One can be used as a selfie stick and can sit on a tabletop. The other can be raised to four feet. It can be used with a cell phone or camera. They're both lightweight, equipped with a Bluetooth remote and easily fit into any carry-on bag.

Once I got over feeling uncomfortable with people staring at me taking my own photos, I got good at it. People are always amazed and offer to help. I learned what angles work for me and all about lighting. I became more natural at posing and knowing which side of my body photographs better.

There are times when using a tripod is inconvenient. The area may be crowded, or the ground may not be leveled or wet. There are some places that don't allow them. When I was visiting the Alcazar in Seville, Spain, I wasn't allowed to put my tripod on the floor in certain areas. I had to get creative by tying my phone to a post or propping it up and asking another tourist to help.

If you need someone to take your photo, ask someone with a camera that's with a group. Chances are they know how to take photos and they're not a thief. Set up your camera or phone for them so they can get the shot the way you want it. Offer to take a photo for them as well. Be careful. There are many thieves and scammers out there just waiting to run away with your camera or phone.

Hiring a photographer is something I have started doing for five years now. It makes it easier to enjoy site seeing and still come home with wonderful pictures. It's not expensive. I take my own photos of landscaping, architecture and statues. I hire a professional to take pictures of me. Expedia, Viator, Airbnb and other tour companies offer freelance photographers as an excursion option. They'll take you around your destination and do a photoshoot of the famous areas and attractions. I use Airbnb a lot because they're solo-friendly. There's no single-person fee. The photographer is a local native of the country.

Hiring a private tour guide is another option. Most of them are excellent at taking pictures. When your tour is private, they only have you to cater to. My guide in Egypt was the best. He took the most amazing pictures, and he knew all types of camera tricks. I hardly used my camera. Mostly all the pictures were taken with my iPhone.

## GETTING AROUND

Getting around is not complicated at all. I usually hire a tour guide during my planning stages. I hire guides that other people have used and referred. Social media travel groups are great to get recommendations for anything travel related. I've had the best experience with travel guides recommended by travel groups. Some guides have packages, and some will customize the trip for you.

The tour guide provides your transportation. A good guide will include entrance fees to tourist attractions and at least a nice lunch daily in your itinerary. You should not have to worry about the cost of things once you get there. Most of all, you don't want the hassle of handling money in crowded areas.

My guide for Egypt was amazing. His name is **Waleed Elakbawy.** You can find him on Facebook. He made sure everything was included. He haggled prices for me. He was my photographer, my protector and today he is my brother. He treated me like a queen. He is so knowledgeable about the history. He has a heart of gold. We stay in touch, and I send all my clients and friends going to Egypt to him. He is registered with the tourism board and is a certified tour guide. Make sure when you hire a guide, they send you copies of their credentials. They should only ask that you send a small deposit if any. The rest should be paid upon arrival.

Another tour guide I must mention is my guide for Cartagena, Columbia. His name is **Freddy Paz**. You can also find him on Facebook. If you want to really experience Cartagena as a solo traveler or a group, Freddy is great. He is very knowledgeable about his country and city. He really loves what he does, and it shows. Cartagena is a party place. Freddie will make sure you have a great time and keep you safe. He always makes sure you're safe, especially in the water. I stay in contact with him as well. Many tour guides that I have used did not return to the travel business post-Covid. These two are holding on strong.

If you're not comfortable hiring a guide prior to your travel, you can always use the hotel concierge to assist you with a driver or taxi. If you like the driver, then negotiate a price for him to drive you daily. Most of them jump at the chance because it's guaranteed income. I do this all the time when I visit the Caribbean islands. It's the best way to see everything. Who better to show you around than a local person? You can really experience the true culture. I have been to some of their homes, met their families and ate delicious home-cooked meals. I've been invited to weddings and parties. In Istanbul, Turkey, my driver's mother made homemade Turkish meatballs for me. They were so delicious. In Morocco, my guide's mother cooked lunch for me, Tagine Chicken. Amazing! Freddy Paz arranged for the tour group to eat at the home of a traditional family home in Palenque. We had such a great time, and the food was outstanding. Many countries have Uber or a similar system. I have not tried it yet.

If you're a free spirit or traveling on a budget, take the metro. The metro systems in Europe are very user-friendly. I grew up in NYC and found London's metro less complicated. Spain also. Both were safe and very clean. There are attendants in the stations to assist you with directions and buying metro cards. Remember to be careful. The metro is a haven for pickpockets, as there are lots of people in close proximity.

Another great way to explore the city is on the hop-on and off buses. Just about every major city offers this to see many attractions in a timely fashion. These buses are specifically for tourists. You can buy a day pass, multiple days or even a week pass. It's up to you. You can ride all around the city and if there's an attraction you want to visit, just hop off at that location. When you finish exploring, get back on another bus to visit another location. Make sure you keep up with the map of the bus lines and ending service time. There are typically schedules for the different seasons.

There are many options of transportation to choose from including renting cars. Make sure you are comfortable with driving on the opposite side of the road and narrow winding streets. I never rent cars out of the USA when I travel solo. I am not comfortable driving alone in a foreign country. The most important thing is that you're comfortable with what you choose. If you're not comfortable with the metro system, be sure to budget for other modes of transportation. The worst thing you can do is be flustered and ruin your vacation.

## EXCURSIONS

Now that you've traveled to your destination, get out and explore! Enjoy the people, the food and the culture. Try something you've never done before, something new and exotic.

In Puerto Morales, Mexico I ate fried grasshoppers. They were sweet and delicious with a nice, cold beer. In Cartagena, I ate fried big red ants. They were okay. There's so much to see and do. Be adventurous or at least step out of your comfort zone.

When I went to Marrakesh, Morocco I hiked up the Atlas Mountain. This was no easy task for me. I'm not a sports person. I'm a girly girl and I don't like to do anything that will cause me to break into a sweat except dancing. I climbed halfway up before my knees said no more. Morocco was the fifth and final country I would visit for my 30-day journey. My knees were tired. A donkey came to my rescue and carried me to the top. Waiting for me was a wonderfully prepared homemade Berber lunch. I was so proud because I tried, and I stepped out of my comfort zone.

In Thailand, I got rid of my fear of snakes. Before traveling to Phuket, Thailand, I couldn't even look at a snake. The thought of touching one made me squeamish. I met two sisters from Australia on an excursion. Amanda and Jessica. The sweetest young ladies. We bonded and spent the day together. We decided to get over our fear of snakes together and share our love for elephants. At an animal farm, I played with a python and let it wrap itself around me. It was a wonderful experience. I refused to let something have that much control over me. I still don't like snakes, but I'm no longer afraid. I respect them and their space.

## Let's Go Take Pictures And Explore

In Dubai, I went sand dunning in the desert. I drove my own-dirt bike. Usually, I would be on the back of someone else's. I also flew in a helicopter with no doors. In Egypt, I took a hot air balloon ride over the Valley of the Kings. It was breathtaking! I was so amazed by the view; I forgot how high up I was in a basket. I'm not saying you must go to this extreme but do something new and totally outside your norm. Skydiving is on my bucket list, but it must be somewhere with an amazing view. Any suggestions?

You don't have to do something every day. Pace yourself and add in time to relax or you'll be exhausted.

Technology has made planning and researching excursions so easy. You don't have to buy books on specific countries or cities anymore. Everything you need to know is online. You don't have to wait in line at the hotel concierge counter unless you choose to. Expedia, Visit-a-City, Trip Advisor, Viator, Airbnb and many more have huge listings of things to do in major cities of any country. You just type in the city and country, the dates you will be visiting and a list of all the available activities will pop up. It shows you the price and all about the excursion. This is a good way to budget for activities for your trip. I suggest you compare the price of different sites. Always read about cancellations, refunds and reviews. This keeps you from wasting time trying to figure it out when you get there. You can pre-plan and prepay for everything. This will allow you to hit the streets as soon as you arrive. The sites also give information about restrictions on age, weight, disabilities and activity levels. Please take the time to read about the activity level. Make sure you're in shape and can endure all the stair climbing and walking that may be involved. Many attractions in Asia and Europe involve stair climbing. If the activity involves water, check to see if must be able to swim and at what level, Beginner, intermediate or strong? Are life jackets included?

In Egypt, the stairs are steep and narrow going into the tombs. Some require bending over while walking down and up the stairs until you reach further in where you will be able to stand.

In Bali, Indonesia I visited several beaches on my last two days. I went to this beautiful beach called Padang Padang. In order to get to the beach, you must walk down many stairs and then to a narrow cave with stairs. Once you arrive, it's the most beautiful view ever. The water is amazing. Going back up is the problem. After laying out in the sun and not properly hydrating myself, it was difficult walking back up. I had to keep stopping to rest.

Please do your research before purchasing your ticket for an excursion. If you're using a tour guide, ask about the activity level of your entire itinerary.

# Let's Go Take Pictures And Explore

CHAPTER 12

# You're On Vacation

*"Traveling—it leaves you speechless, then turns you into a storyteller."*
**IBN Battuta**

After all your planning and worrying you've reached your destination. You did it! You traveled solo! Now enjoy yourself. Relax. Enjoy every moment. Allow yourself the opportunity to get to know yourself and love yourself. Let go of all the negative thoughts and embrace each moment with positivity and excitement. Get lost and indulge in the culture. Indulge in you.

I come back a little different with every vacation. I'm wiser, more patient, confident, invigorated and a better me. I'm happy to return home to see my family and friends. I enjoy organizing and reviewing photos of the wonderful time I had and the beautiful people I met along the way. I'm barely unpacked before I start thinking and planning my next adventure.

It's time to stop waiting on people to go on vacation with you. You're missing out on the chance to make enjoyable memories, meet new friends and fall deeply in love with yourself. Solo travel may not be for everyone, but everyone should try it at least once. I must warn you; it can be very addicting. I'd rather travel by myself than with anyone else.

*"You will never be alone if you like the person, you're with!"*

# About The Author

Sandra Denise Parker, affectionately known as "Queen", is a free spirit, fun-loving, adventurous and ambitious woman who has never met a stranger. She loves to help people shine and be the best they can be.

After using solo travel as a means to help her learn to face her fears and deeply love herself, she is now a transformational life coach and motivational speaker. She specializes in self-love, chakra healing and leadership. She coaches women on the importance of self-love, self-care and chakra healing to obtain optimal health of the mind, body and spirit.

She assists women with working through their fears and teaches them how to embrace their divine feminine energy to facilitate self-love in order to acquire their lifelong goals and dreams. She believes self-love is the master key to living a life of purpose and fulfillment.

# On My Own

Born and raised in Brooklyn, New York, she now resides in South Carolina. Sandra takes pride in being a mother, grandmother, registered nurse and nurse leader for almost 30 years. She is a world traveler and the CEO of Pac-n-Play Travel, a concierge travel service and blog. She is also the CEO and founder of Queen Thangz, LLC, a company she established to enhance the queen in women through semiprecious stone handmade jewelry, accessories and life coaching services.

Sandra is a dynamic speaker and orator with an amazing story and the ability to touch people's hearts and souls.

All inquiries for coaching or speaking engagements can be addressed to:

Email: Sandra@coachingwithqueen.com
      www.coachingwithqueen.com
Email: https://pacnplay.com for travel inquiries.

# Acknowledgments

I would like to thank everyone who continuously encouraged me to share and write about my travel experiences. You're the reason I had the courage to write this book. A big thank you with hugs and kisses to Allison Turnley and Patti Oliverio for always fixing the schedule at work to allow many requests for days off for my travel adventures.

Thank you to Cassandra Burch, my spiritual mother who stands by me and cheers me on with unconditional love. To my friend Laura Johson-Nazon, who pushes me to be the best that I can be and believed in me when I didn't believe in myself. Thank you so much for investing in me and teaching me the importance of investing in myself.

I would also like to thank Natasa Denman and the team at the Ultimate 48 Hour Author for making the book publishing process so smooth even through me overthinking everything.

Finally, I would like to thank everyone who purchases or reads this book. It's a labor of love and I hope it helps you on your self-love journey and gets you started as a solo traveler.

Be Sure to

Download Your

Free Gift

@ coachingwithqueen.com

Check out my beautiful jewelry at https://queenthangz.com

Let's be friends:

Instagram @Queenthangz_ for self-love inspiration

Facebook @Sandra Gemini- Queen Parker

Instagram @Geminiqueentravels to keep up with my latest travel adventures.

# Notes

**On My Own**

# Notes

www.ingramcontent.com/pod-product-compliance
Lightning Source LLC
Chambersburg PA
CBHW040241130526
44590CB00049B/4139